Swamplife

SWAMPLIFE

People, Gators, and Mangroves
Entangled in the Everglades

Laura A. Ogden

A Quadrant Book

UNIVERSITY OF MINNESOTA PRESS
MINNEAPOLIS
LONDON

Quadrant, a joint initiative of the University of Minnesota Press and the Institute for
Advanced Study at the University of Minnesota, provides support for interdisciplinary
scholarship within a new, more collaborative model of research and publication.

QUADRANT Sponsored by Quadrant's Environment, Culture, and Sustainability group (advisory
board: Bruce Braun, Christine Marran, and Dan Philippon) and by the Institute on the
Environment at the University of Minnesota.

Quadrant is generously funded by the Andrew W. Mellon Foundation.

http://quadrant.umn.edu

Chapter 5 was previously published as "Searching for Paradise in the Florida Everglades," *Cultural Geographies* 15, no. 2 (2008): 207–29; reprinted by permission of Sage
Publications, Inc.; all rights reserved.

Published by the University of Minnesota Press
111 Third Avenue South, Suite 290
Minneapolis, MN 55401-2520
http://www.upress.umn.edu

Library of Congress Cataloging-in-Publication Data
Ogden, Laura A.
  Swamplife : people, gators, and mangroves entangled in the Everglades /
Laura A. Ogden.
     p.   cm.
  A Quadrant Book.
  Includes bibliographical references and index.
  ISBN 978-0-8166-7026-0 (hc : alk. paper)
  ISBN 978-0-8166-7027-7 (pb : alk. paper)
  1. Human ecology — Florida — Everglades National Park. 2. Mangrove
ecology — Florida — Everglades National Park. 3. Everglades National Park (Fla.) —
Social conditions. 4. Everglades National Park (Fla.) — Environmental conditions.
I. Title.
  GF504.F6O44   2011
  577.69'8270975939 — dc22   2011003346

Printed in the United States of America on acid-free paper

The University of Minnesota is an equal-opportunity educator and employer.

18 17 16 15 14   10 9 8 7 6 5 4

CONTENTS

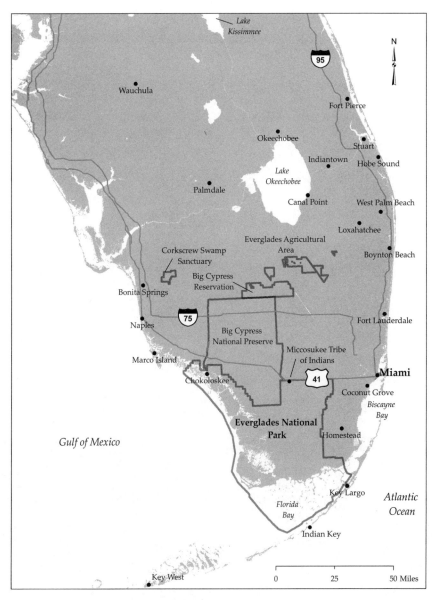

Southern Florida and the Greater Everglades Watershed

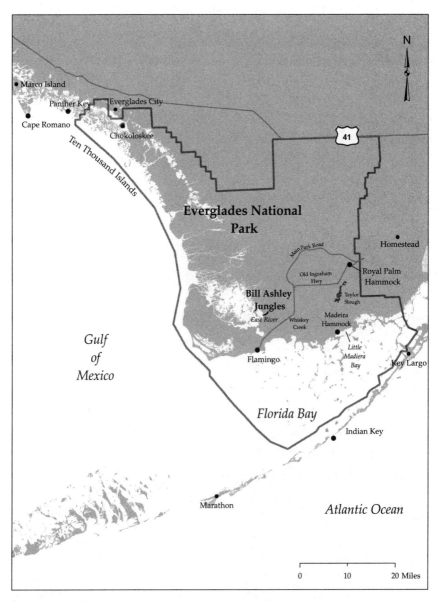

Everglades National Park

ACKNOWLEDGMENTS

The fieldwork for this book began more than a decade ago. Between 1996 and 1997, I conducted an oral history project with Glen Simmons that documented his experiences as an alligator hunter in the southern Everglades during the early part of the twentieth century. The University Press of Florida published the results of this fieldwork in 1998 in the book *Gladesmen: Alligator Hunters, Moonshiners, and Skiffers.* Simmons began the process of writing a book early in his lifetime: beginning in the 1940s, he jotted down observations ("hundreds of curlew on Joe River Camp"), funny sayings, and hunting records in small pocket-sized ledgers. He then transferred these notes into stacks of larger, spiral-bound notebooks that he gave to me. I used the notebooks as starting points for an almost daily, yearlong interview. We took many trips together into the backcountry, searching out the sites of former hunting camps, me sitting in the bow of a gladeskiff while he poled us through the dense saw grass marshes. When Simmons tired, I would wade through the waist-high waters, scanning for alligators, as I pulled the boat along. Other days we spent scrambling over and under the tangled prop roots of the mangrove swamps, a difficult feat for a nearly blind man, seeking the sites where moonshiners' stills had once been hidden. On these trips, Simmons taught me more than the human history of the area. From him I learned how to interpret nature's subtle signs—the meaning of alligator scat and deer tracks, and the beauty of fresh growth after a fire. Certainly, this book would not have been written without the support of Simmons and his wife, Maxie.

Other ethnographic material in this book derives from two projects that I participated in while under contract with the Florida Department of State,

Division of Historic Resources. In 1998, I was involved with a broad survey of traditional folklife in southern Florida, with my research focusing specifically on coastal and Everglades culture. I conducted ethnographic interviews with commercial and recreational fishermen as well as with Seminole artisans living on the Big Cypress and Hollywood reservations. Research from that project was presented as a traveling museum exhibition. The following year I completed six months of fieldwork for a "Swamp Culture" research project, also funded by the state of Florida, and worked in the village of Palmdale (within the Fisheating Creek swamp area), the community of Corkscrew (within the Corkscrew Swamp), and in Everglades City and Chokoloskee (island towns within the Ten Thousand Islands). I interviewed former alligator hunters, commercial fishermen, frog and turtle hunters, and families associated with traditional Everglades tourism. During this second research project, I met H. Pete Whidden of Corkscrew, who graciously allowed me to interview him on several occasions. Like Simmons's recollections, Whidden's voice emerges as a central narrative within this book. I thank him for his time and patience, and I recognize that without his insights (as well as those from all the others who let me into their lives), this book would not have been possible. While working on these projects, I received ample guidance and support from my colleagues Bob Stone, an independent scholar and ethnomusicologist, and Tina Bucuvalas, state folklorist with the Florida Folklife Program. Bob and Tina are terrific collaborators and substantially contributed to my emerging skills as an ethnographer.

Much of this book is historical, written at the time when discourses of Everglades ecosystem restoration planning and implementation shape our understandings and attitudes toward the Everglades. My insights into ecosystem-restoration planning began with a two-year contract with the Governor's Commission for a Sustainable South Florida, a multiagency and community-planning organization established by former governor Lawton Chiles in 1994. As a commission staff member, my primary job was to work with other social scientists to develop a research agenda for Everglades restoration planning and implementation. I have written elsewhere about the commission's work and my involvement with restoration planning, and I am exceedingly grateful to Barbara Rose Johnston and Bonnie Kranzer for their guidance and for the opportunities that this work afforded me to experience, firsthand, the politics of nature that are transforming the contemporary Everglades.

My collaborators at the National Science Foundation's Long-Term Ecological Research Program (LTER) have been fundamental to my understandings of ecological theory. The LTER program provided an intellectually challenging and open environment to discuss and debate the humanity of ecology and environmental change. In particular, I express my gratitude to Dan Childers, Morgan Grove, and Ted Gragson: they welcomed my skepticism and propelled my greater participation in network-level LTER science planning and teaching. Locally, the Florida Coastal Everglades LTER program (FCE LTER), based at Florida International University, has provided a critical scholarly community for my research. This research was enhanced by collaborations with the Florida Coastal Everglades Long-Term Ecological Research program (funded by the National Science Foundation DBI-0620409 and DEB-9910514). Though I continue to be amazed and impressed at the level of collaboration among all the scholars at FCE LTER, I particularly thank Evelyn Gaiser, René Price, Jeff Onsted, Rinku Roy Chowdhury, Hugh Gladwin, Jim Heffernan, and Rebecca Garvoille.

Several colleagues were instrumental in the writing of this book. I express my appreciation to Becky Zarger, Rod Neumann, Andrew Mathews, and Juliet Erazo: these dear friends each provided thoughtful comments at various stages of this manuscript's development. Paul Robbins and Jessica Cattelino served as (once) anonymous reviewers; their thoughtful and thorough comments substantially contributed to the book's revisions, and I am sincerely grateful for their interventions. I also acknowledge and thank the faculty, particularly Bruce Braun and Jean Langford, at the Quadrant program, a collaboration between the University of Minnesota's Institute for Advanced Study and the University of Minnesota Press, for supportive engagement with this book's ideas. Jason Weidemann of the University of Minnesota Press has been a tremendously helpful editor, and I am very grateful for his collaboration on this project.

Deborah Mitchell is a wonderful photographer, and her images offer a lovely counterpoint to the text. Tony Oliver-Smith served as my dissertation chair during a time when many of these ideas began to take form; his warm enthusiasm then and subsequent mentorship over the years continue to offer inspiration. Mary Free's incisive touch in editing this manuscript was immeasurably helpful. Finally, I acknowledge the tremendous debt I owe Gail Hollander. During the past several years, she has spent endless hours reading manuscripts, rereading the same manuscripts, talking about ideas, and helping me negotiate the tricky path to tenure. In the process, Gail and her husband, Rod Neumann, have become members of my extended family.

This book would not have been possible without the support of my immediate family. My father, John Ogden, and his wife, Maryanne, have spent their lives as keen observers of the Everglades. Living only three miles down the road from us, they are always on hand to share a glass of wine and talk about the Everglades and restoration as well as to share their love of the outdoors with my daughter. My mother, Mary Ann Bolla, was an incomparable collector of rare manuscripts on Everglades natural history. She died unexpectedly while I was writing this book. My mother's holistic knowledge and enthusiasm for all things Everglades can be found throughout this book, which I finish with profound sadness: she should be here to celebrate with us. In all the joy and heartache of the past several years, my husband, Pat, has kept our family on course and laughing. For this, and thousands of other reasons, I dedicate this book to him.

1. THE FLORIDA EVERGLADES
An Entangled Landscape

As a landscape, the Everglades has epitomized all that we think of as nature at its most uncultivated: an icon infested with frightening reptiles, botanical excess, swarms of mosquitoes, and unforgiving heat. This is the alien and impenetrable Everglades that stymied the attempts of early surveyors and settlers and that continues to provide dramatic flair to countless novels, films, and other accounts of swampland exploration. At the same time, these exotic visions of the landscape have supported widespread practices of landscape transformation, particularly schemes of drainage and development, as they have in the swamps and wetlands throughout the Americas.[1] In southern Florida, beginning in the late 1800s, the sense that the value of the Everglades lay solely in its potential for "reclamation" and cultivation led to the drainage and development of two-thirds of the historic Everglades. Yet even as the dredging machines plowed forward, in their slow bid to create canals through the muck, concerned scientists and citizens lobbied to protect a landscape they considered both unique and fragile. Certainly this protectionist, and increasingly ecologized, vision has gained momentum over the past thirty years, culminating in today's multibillion-dollar plans for Everglades restoration.

Today, all these visions of the Everglades have become entangled into a set of contradictory practices and politics of nature. Yet within this entanglement, the place of people in the Everglades remains highly ambivalent. For the most part, humanity in the Everglades has been displaced to roles of externalized agents of change, with most accounts focused on conflicts over its drainage and resources. The narrative arc of these accounts generally begins with the landscape's settlement and drainage in the mid-nineteenth

An abandoned camp in the Big Cypress Swamp.
Photograph by Deborah Mitchell.

century, then details the ensuing environmental devastation, and ends with a triumphant plea for restoration. In these narratives, the Everglades is an unpeopled landscape that humans act upon. As a corrective to this selective vision, this book reclaims the landscape as a place of people and human history. But I do so with a particular interest in understanding how what it means to be "human" is constituted through changing relations with other animals, plants, material objects, and the like.

This book focuses on the world-making practices of poor rural whites, called gladesmen, alligators, snakes, mangroves, and fire (this book's central characters). Gladesmen settled in southern Florida at the midpoint of the nineteenth century. They and their descendents supported themselves primarily through commercial and subsistence hunting and fishing and through small-scale farming. Although this has been an Everglades history largely neglected by scholars, there is a robust popular literature that tends to both romanticize and essentialize rural Everglades life into easy stories of outlaws and outsiders. Certainly this outlaw mythology has become an important part of what the Everglades is and means — including to gladesmen themselves. For this reason, I return again and again to stories of the most famous Everglades outlaws, the Ashley Gang. Still, these outlaw stories contribute little to our sense of the Everglades as a real human experience, one emerging out of specific relations among hunters and the nonhuman world. More problematically, Everglades lore, with its ever-present simplified "outlaw" (poacher, moonshiner, gangster, and so on), blinds us to a critical appreciation of how oppositional culture and social class operate in our understandings of wilderness in the United States.

As the Everglades became increasingly transformed by drainage and development projects throughout the late nineteenth and early twentieth centuries, the calls to protect remnant wild lands gained political and social acceptance. This lobbying for Everglades protection and conservation recalls the romanticism inherent to the creation of wilderness throughout the United States.[2] In particular, this wilderness paradigm reverberated with Edenic overtones that positioned rural inhabitants of wild lands as uncivilized threats to nature's purity.[3] Rural whites, in contrast to indigenous peoples, were particularly suspect. In these Everglades wilderness stories, indigenous Seminoles and Miccosukees of southern Florida are discursively and simplistically sited within the landscape. Certainly, the nature–Native metonym entails multiple racist effacements, including, in the case of the Seminoles and Miccosukees, a history of resisting genocidal removal practices, pressures on land and resources, and current efforts to maintain their territorial and tribal autonomy. At the same time, Native presence (both precolonial and contemporary) in the Everglades is accorded an acceptability that is not extended to rural poor whites. As I argue in this book, the displacement of rural white hunters from the Everglades reflects their unsettled class positioning; these hunters were petty commodity traders whose livelihoods stood in stark contrast to Florida's prevailing identity as a tourist and agricultural empire.

The story of gladesmen in the Everglades is a story I tell because it is personal. More than a decade ago, Glen Simmons, who was like a grandfather to me, asked me to help him write a book about his experiences growing up in the Everglades.[4] Throughout my childhood, I spent weekends and summers with Glen and his wife, Maxie, at their home on the outskirts of Everglades National Park. My family celebrated Christmas and other holidays with the Simmonses—often picnicking in the park. As I grew older, they supported and encouraged me when I was in college and graduate school. So when Glen asked me to help him write a book, I immediately agreed. I started the book project interested in documenting the drastic environmental changes to the Everglades that Glen had witnessed in his lifetime; he was born in 1916 and remembered an Everglades that was vastly different from the Everglades of my lifetime. The rapid pace of development and the related drastic reduction of Everglades wildlife caused him great sorrow and fueled his anger. During the course of the interviews for the book, I was surprised to find that for most of Glen's life, he had been a commercial alligator hunter. I did not know this because he never talked about it. Certainly some of his friends and family were aware of this past. But for the most part, Glen was reticent about it. His reticence stemmed from the fact that alligator hunting in Florida was illegal and had been for most of his life. In many ways, I have written this book to understand the processes by which his history and experiences of the Everglades became marginalized, illegal, and largely forgotten. I refer to these processes of displacement as the "politics of nature."

I write this book at a time when these displacements continue to hold sway over ideas and practices toward the Everglades even though they are reconstituted in new forms. Our contemporary Everglades is at the center of the highly politicized restoration effort. In response to the massive ecological problems caused by reengineering and development practices in southern Florida, the U.S. Congress authorized the Comprehensive Everglades Restoration Plan (CERP) in 2000. Spanning 18,000 square miles, with costs estimated to rise beyond current projections of $19.7 billion, the Everglades restoration program is certainly one of the most comprehensive environmental projects ever attempted.[5] The restoration effort is guided, in part, by principles of ecosystem management, reflecting the popularity of ecosystem approaches within U.S. environmental mitigation and conservation efforts as well as in academic ecological studies. In theory, the ecosystem, as a heuristic for ordering knowledge about the world, seeks to systematically integrate humans with nonhuman nature.[6] In practice, such approaches tend to disarticulate the humanity of nature by focusing solely on anthropogenic "stressors" to ecological systems or by conceptualizing humans as externalized beneficiaries of the ecosystem's services. This has certainly been the case within the context of Everglades restoration, as I have argued elsewhere.[7]

In no way would I suggest that people have not permanently transformed the southern Florida environment. In my lifetime, I have witnessed development schemes that threaten the quality of life of *all* the inhabitants of the Everglades, including its peoples. Yet displacing human history and contemporary landscape practices to a place of externalized difference remains a losing proposition. Without a more humanized and nuanced politics of nature, we cannot hope to create (or imagine) sustainable futures. This book seeks to redress these monocular visions by exploring the shifting, multiple, and often asymmetrical relations among people, plants, reptiles, and water, among other elements, that are the Everglades. In doing so, this book problematizes paradigms of wilderness and ecosystems that continue to shape our understandings of the Everglades and to drive conservation and development policies around the world.

The displacement of gladesmen from the Everglades is hardly the only story of cultural marginalization and displacement important to our understanding of the landscape. Indigenous people have lived in southern Florida for over 10,000 years, well before the environment at all resembled the Everglades of today. As I discuss below, very few of the original indigenous people of the Everglades survived Florida's Spanish colonial period. During the early decades of the nineteenth century, wars with the United States and U.S. practices of deportation reduced the number of contemporary Seminoles living in the Everglades to only a few hundred survivors. And the story of rural, poor whites in the Everglades is intimately bound up with these histories. I remember a man telling me in an interview that his family had moved into southern Florida *only* after the Indian wars had made it safe for them to do so. White settlement in southern Florida brought increased pressure on Seminole hunting and fishing stocks, further jeopardizing Seminole livelihoods. The rest of this chapter sketches the imbricating processes of displacement that produced the modern Everglades and that are a critical lens for understanding the gladesmen's Everglades.

DEPOPULATION, DEPORTATIONS AND RESISTANCE

When the Spanish arrived in Florida in 1513, there were over 20,000 Native people living in the greater Everglades region, the majority and most powerful of whom were Calusas, who lived along the southwest coast.[8] The southern Florida indigenous societies that the Spanish encountered, named "Glades Culture" by archaeologists, were prosperous and socially complex. The memoirs and related documents of Hernando de Escalante Fontaneda, who was a captive of the Calusa for seventeen years, provides the most comprehensive description of colonial-era indigenous society in Florida.[9] Fontaneda estimated that there were about fifty indigenous towns loosely networked into a tribute-paying political hierarchy.[10] The Calusas (as well as the people who lived for a few thousand years before the Calusas) built dramatic shell mounds and earthworks throughout the southwestern coastal areas of Florida. These earthworks were built in varied configurations that served multiple purposes; they included horseshoe-shaped protective jetties, inland transportation canals, and elevated plateaus used as village sites. Chokoloskee Island, a coastal fishing village, exemplifies the last type of earthwork. Chokoloskee is built on a 150-acre shell mound that is twenty feet high in places, the largest such mound in the southeastern United States. Less noticeably but equally significant, evidence of several thousand years of human use can be found on almost all the tree islands within the Everglades freshwater sloughs and marshes. We are only now beginning to consider the legacy of these intentional transformations of the landscape on the ecology and evolution of the contemporary Everglades.

Spanish contact with Florida's indigenous populations resulted in their near total annihilation throughout the state.[11] In the Everglades, the Spanish colonial period was an era of rapid Native depopulation and cultural change. The Calusas, and other indigenous groups, engaged in trade, obtaining metal goods and tools from the Spanish; many became Christian and learned to speak Spanish, and they famously captured, enslaved, and often sacrificed the survivors of Spanish shipwrecks. With these interactions came the spread of diseases to which Everglades Native peoples had little immunity, such as measles and smallpox, and increased intertribal warfare and other forms of cultural disruption. In a letter to Queen Mariana of Spain written in 1675, the bishop of Cuba, Gabriel Díaz Vara Calderón, described the people living along the "Coast of the Southern Frontier" as "13 tribes of savage heathen Carib Indians, in camps, having no fixed abodes, living only on fish and roots of trees."[12] In other words, by the midpoint of the first Spanish colonial period, these once powerful and prosperous Everglades tribes were living in scattered groups with scant material evidence to indicate their prior rich spiritual and economic life. Within another hundred years, almost all the Glades Culture–era people were gone from the Everglades, with most of the remaining families reportedly boarding Spanish ships for Havana in 1763.[13]

For the next several decades the Everglades was largely deserted. Some Native peoples who survived Florida's colonial period may have held on in isolated camps, and there are reports of Cuban fishermen and "Spanish Indians" along the Everglades coast during this time. Certainly there are considerable gaps in our understanding of the human history of the Everglades during Florida's Spanish, English, and French colonial periods. But it seems very likely that Everglades indigenous groups who survived Florida's colonial and early-American periods (Calusas, Tequestas, and others) may have united with indigenous groups who were being pushed southward into Florida's peninsula from Georgia, Alabama, and northern Florida. Still, for

The author's husband and daughter stand atop a Calusa shell mound on the Turner River. Photograph by author.

the most part, for a brief period in time, the Everglades was largely depopulated and abandoned.

Contemporary Seminoles in southern Florida trace their ancestry through 12,000 years of indigenous history in the southeastern United States. Originally living in Creek Confederacy towns in the southeast, indigenous people now known as the Seminoles moved into Spanish northern Florida in the early eighteenth century.[14] Living in northern Florida, this amalgam of southeastern Indians, as well as descendents of African American slaves, practiced traditional town-based agriculture and raised livestock.[15] Expanding European and later American presence in northern and central Florida forcibly dislocated the Seminoles multiple times — including with the deportation of a majority of the population to Indian Territory in Oklahoma during the mid-1800s.[16] The few hundred Seminoles who remained moved southward into the Everglades and the Big Cypress Swamp. Here they lived in dispersed extended-family matrilineal "camps" and practiced small-field horticulture and hunting. As the archaeologist Frank Griffin notes, the camp settlement pattern grew out of a need for mobility and practices of guerrilla warfare, yet it proved to be a remarkable adaptation to the Everglades environment.[17] From early on, Seminole hunters participated in the commercial hide market, selling alligator hides and otter pelts at trading posts in Fort Lauderdale, Miami, and other locations, as well as engaging in subsistence hunting for deer and other animals.

The first Americans to explore the Everglades interior were probably soldiers participating in the Second Seminole War (1835–1842), one of a series of bloody conflicts that Andrew Jackson initiated to forcibly remove the Seminoles from Florida. In fact, an anonymous soldier who participated in these wars wrote the oldest known account of an American crossing the southern Everglades. The soldier was part of a military raiding party led by Colonel William S. Harney during the winter of 1840.[18] On this trip, Harney led ninety men in sixteen canoes from Fort Dallas, located on the northern bank of the Miami River, to track the famed Seminole leader Chekika to his backcountry camp in the southern Everglades. The historian Charlton Tebeau describes Harney as "willingly accepting" this assignment, his enthusiasm spurred by a desire to avenge Chekika's early-morning raid on

George Osceola skinning an alligator at an unidentified Seminole camp, August 1907.
Photograph by Julian Dimock; printed by permission of the American Museum of Natural History.

Indian Key during the summer of 1840. Chekika's attack at Indian Key, a settlement of about fifty people halfway down the island chain, resulted in the deaths of Dr. Henry Perrine and six others who lived there.[19] John T. Sprague's account of the Seminole Wars, published originally in 1848, includes a detailed description of the Indian Key massacre. Throughout the attack, Perrine's wife and two children hid themselves, partially underwater, in a small turtle-crawl located under the floor of their stilt house. The family hunkered down in their confined space for many hours, listening as Dr. Perrine was killed in a room above; afterward they were almost buried in the marl as the house burned around them.[20]

For these soldiers, crossing the Everglades was a daunting and difficult task. In the soldiers' words, the Everglades was "like a vast sea, filled with grass and green trees," bearing little resemblance to anything they had previously encountered.[21] Though the Everglades was terra incognita to the soldiers, the American military was well aware that the Seminoles knew the Everglades interior intimately. To compensate for this tactical advantage, the American soldiers engaged in multiple transformations to become Indian, or at least their version of Indian. The soldiers dressed themselves as Seminoles, used canoes to negotiate the landscape, and camped on the same inland islands the Seminoles used, as had prehistoric Native people before them. After surprising Chekika and the families who were camped with him at his backcountry camp, a soldier named Hall chased Chekika through the woods, killed him, then scalped him and hung the great warrior from a tree. In penetrating this Indian landscape, the soldiers felt they had "accomplished what [had] never been done by white man."[22]

By 1858, at the close of the Third Seminole War, the population of Seminoles living in southern Florida had dwindled to about two hundred.[23] These survivors tended to avoid contact with settlers, instead staying in their village camps. Here, the Seminoles grew sugarcane, corn, sweet potatoes, and other vegetables; fished; and hunted for wild birds, deer, alligators, and other animals. The decades after the war brought increased white settlement in the northern Everglades around Lake Okeechobee and along the southeastern and southwestern coasts. Over time, complex reciprocal relations grew between white settlers and some Seminoles, particularly Seminoles involved in the hide, plume, and pelt trade. As Harry Kersey notes, during the last quarter of the nineteenth century, it was the settlers and their families who ran trading posts who were closest to the Seminoles.[24] It was to these outposts, such as Ted Smallwood's store in Chokoloskee or Brown's Boat Landing in the Big Cypress, that Seminoles came to sell alligator hides and plume feathers in exchange for guns, ammunition, calico, ribbons, pots and pans, sewing machines, and other dry goods.[25] Although these trading relationships fostered complex reciprocal dependencies, and even friendships, for the most part, increased white settlement in the Everglades led to escalating friction and pressure on tribal lands.[26]

RECLAIMING THE SWAMP

Charles B. Vignoles, an Irish-born civil engineer, appears to have been, in 1823, the first to refer to the swamps of southern Florida as "Ever-glades," reflecting the landscape's vastness.[27] Whether as soldiers, explorers, or surveyors, Americans encountering the Everglades during the middle to late 1800s were simply overwhelmed by its spatial extent. Major Archie Williams led the first expedition to cross the Everglades from north to south in 1883 on a trip funded by the *New Orleans Times-Democrat* newspaper. Williams's first impressions of the great Everglades prairies south of Lake Okeechobee portray a landscape of unrelenting, unlimited sameness:

> Again and again we bring into use our field glass, but alas, the same unbroken level plain meets our view, the same brown color unrelieved by even a patch of green or depression or rising in the surface. We are unable to distinguish where the marsh grass ends and the sawgrass begins, for it is all alike, all the same color, the same height, and what is worse still, all the same difficulties and perhaps greater for the next ten miles in our front, on our left and on our right.[28]

Although those who encountered the Everglades in the 1800s may not have always appreciated the ecological diversity of the landscape, their emphasis on its vastness was not exaggerated. Estimates suggest that the pre-drainage Everglades spanned 10,890 square miles and was dominated, as it still is, by prairies of gray green saw grass, named aptly for the razor-like cut inflicted when the plant is rubbed top to bottom.

The Everglades seems deceptively concrete from a distance, yet its underlying element is water. The Seminoles referred to the Everglades as *Pa hay okee*, which translates to "grassy water." This grassy water is only a few inches deep in places; in other areas, it is waist-high. Though early American explorers often commented on the landscape's "monotony," ecologically rich tree-covered islands, called hammocks, punctuate this vast expanse.[29]

The predrainage inland glades then gave way to a band of coastal mangrove swamps, twenty miles wide in places.

Negative ideas about the Everglades were insufficient to deter further Euro-American settlement and attempts at transforming the landscape through drainage. Settlement in the Everglades was bound up in the nation's larger political and economic history and the state's territorial claims. When Florida gained statehood in 1845, much of the southern portion of the state was underwater for periods of the year, and according to federal law, these wetlands remained under the control of the U.S. government. At that time, when agricultural production was considered a national security interest, wetlands were seen as impediments to the developmental interests of the nation.[30] The federal Swamp and Overflowed Land Act of 1850 provided a mechanism for transferring wetlands to states, though this transfer was contingent upon the lands being "reclaimed" for agricultural production. In southern Florida, drainage schemes sputtered along until 1881, at which time Florida governor William Bloxham sold Philadelphia millionaire Hamilton Disston 4 million acres of Everglades land. As part of this deal, and subsequent deals with other investors, Disston was granted ownership of half of any lands his company successfully drained. Disston's efforts were fairly successful; in little over a decade he drained over 50,000 acres of land and created the first major drainage canals in the region. Needless to say, other entrepreneurs quickly followed his lead.[31]

Without reclamation, the Everglades was considered miasmic, dangerous, uncivilized, and certainly worthless. Unleashing the value of this "derelict landscape," as David McCally has termed it,[32] required a new vision of the landscape, one we might understand as "opportunistic." On the one hand, this opportunism was clearly economic. In his treatise *Truck Farming in the Everglades,* published in 1910, Walter Waldin boldly advised, "Nowhere can an individual start a business, agricultural or otherwise, with less cash than right here in South Florida, and nowhere can the agriculturalist find a better place to invest his money."[33] On the other hand, this vision of the Everglades also resonated with less tangible promises, such as that a person might make a "fresh start" within an exotic landscape. In a sales brochure published in 1914 by the Okeechobee Fruit Lands Company, we witness the emergence of this new vision:

If you are not making a financial success in your present environment; if your health requires a perfect climate; or if you are sick of the drudgery of a futureless career at an office desk, come to this *land of opportunity* and settle on America's richest soil. . . . Among those people who have never visited this region there prevails an erroneous conception of its character. It is pictured as a wild, almost impenetrable swamp hidden beneath vine-laden trees—the haunt of snakes, alligators and other reptiles. Instead of these forbidding conditions, the visitor is surprised to see, extending from Lake Okeechobee to Biscayne Bay, a great, almost unbroken stretch of land, in appearance similar to the great plains of the Middle West.[34]

Realizing the potential of this opportune land entailed mammoth efforts at reengineering the landscape, instigated both by the giants of capitalism, such as Henry Flagler, who built the first railroads into southern Florida, and by thousands of struggling settlers, who quickly found that the land's productive potential was not so easily claimed.[35]

The Okeechobee Fruit Lands Company's explicit boosterism was merely a single note in the cacophony that led thousands to buy Florida swampland sight unseen. Specially chartered buses and trains brought northeastern investors into the Miami area; on their arrival, real estate agents immediately bombarded these prospective clients with cheap land deals.[36] By 1924, both the price of land and the number of building permits issued in Miami skyrocketed, ranking it well above other southern cities in real estate development.[37] The 1920s real estate boom brought about a rapid transformation of the landscape, with hundreds of acres of mangrove forests, scrubby pinelands, and inland hammocks being cleared for development. Drainage and development efforts continued at a stuttering pace, with devastating hurricanes and the Great Depression temporarily slowing these schemes.

Early drainage efforts pale in comparison to the water management practices of the mid-twentieth century. During the 1920s two disastrous hurricanes struck the farming communities around Lake Okeechobee. In 1926, 13,000 homes and farms were destroyed along the lake's eastern edge, and over 400 people were left dead.[38] Two years later, another hurricane struck the region, causing the earthen dike around the lake to fail. In an hour's time,

Vintage postcard showing a dredge boat, the *Dredge Miami*, digging a canal through the Everglades.

over 2,000 people, many of them African American farm workers, were drowned by the lake's rushing waters.[39] The public outcry over these tragedies, compounded by devastating floods in the following years that severely impeded the region's agricultural industry, spurred the national government to intercede in southern Florida water management. In 1948, the federal government authorized an ambitious flood control and water management project known as the Central and Southern Florida Project (C & SF Project).

The C & SF Project, constructed by the U.S. Army Corps of Engineers, transformed the Everglades into a highly mechanized plumbing system. It includes one thousand miles of levees and canals, fifteen square miles of interconnected water reservoirs, 150 water control structures, and sixteen major pumping stations. Implementation of the C & SF Project continues today, providing flood control and water delivery to the region's residents, farms, and businesses. Without the C & SF Project, much of modern southern Florida would simply be uninhabitable, particularly during the rainy season, though balancing flood control and water supply has not been simple. To provide adequate flood control for the region, each day water managers divert an average of 1.7 billion gallons of freshwater to the oceans and bays. Diverting water like this causes repeated water shortages and saltwater intrusion to the aquifer.

Owing largely to the success of the C & SF Project, there is little about the contemporary Everglades water cycles that is natural. Although this flood control and drainage facilitated the region's dramatic urban and agricultural development, it also led to widespread changes to Everglades ecology and wildlife. For instance, ornithological records suggest that the region's famous wading bird populations have been reduced by 90 to 95 percent since the predrainage era.[40] This loss is as much historically as ecologically significant, as it was the region's rookeries that first lured naturalists to the area, establishing the Everglades as a landscape of scientific significance. Most dramatic has been the development of two-thirds of the Everglades. This loss of land has been particularly critical to larger mammals, such as the endangered Florida panther, which requires vast habitats for breeding. In all, sixty-eight native Everglades plant and animal species are listed as endangered or threatened.

These landscape transformations hardly followed a linear trajectory from worthless swamp to agro-industrial complex. Instead, as Gail Hollander richly demonstrates, attitudes toward the Everglades have always been highly ambivalent, fraught with contradictions, and bound up in the national and global political economy.[41] As the dredging machines plowed forward, concerned citizens and scientists lobbied relentlessly for the protection of local landscapes and wildlife in the Everglades.[42] Responding to this pressure, federal and state agencies initiated a parallel, through contradictory, approach to managing the Everglades. During the height of state-sponsored drainage initiatives, governmental funding and programs were directed toward the conservation of remnant portions of the Everglades. For instance, in 1947, the year before Congress authorized the C & SF Project, land was set aside for the establishment of Everglades National Park. These policy contradictions embody well-known Western traditions bifurcating

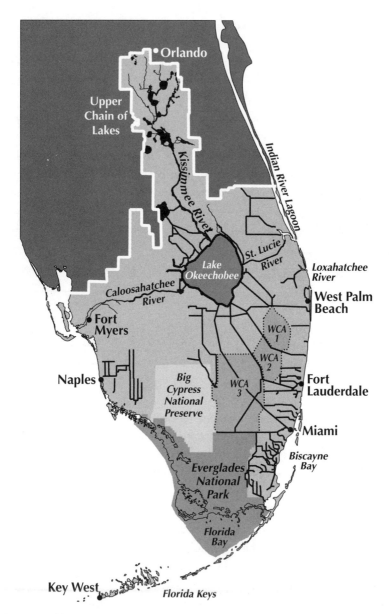

Southern Florida, with lighter-shaded areas indicating the spatial extent of the Everglades Restoration Program. Courtesy of the South Florida Water Management District.

"natural" and "human" landscapes. In southern Florida, drained and developed portions of the Everglades (manifestations of culture and progress) were managed to meet the region's increasing water demand and flood control needs, while less altered areas were treated as uninhabited "wilderness" and were managed to protect native habitat and species.

GLADESMEN OF THE FLORIDA EVERGLADES

Today, 7.5 million people live within the historical Everglades watershed. The region encompasses vast expanses of agricultural farmland (such as the Everglades Agricultural Area, or EAA) and rural towns, as well as a sprawling metropolitan eastern corridor that culminates in the city of Miami. Southern Florida is well known for its steady and increasing population growth, high percentages of elderly and seasonal residents, and neighborhoods and communities where Spanish-speaking residents constitute the majority (such as Miami–Dade County). Drive an hour in any direction across southern Florida, and one cannot help but be struck by the disparity between the obvious excesses of conspicuous consumption (Hummer stretch limousines, gated communities that redefine the notion of exclusivity) and economic vulnerability (rural migrant work camps, block after block of plywood-shuttered houses and storefronts throughout the urban centers).

Yet this book's stories are far removed from the bustling urban sprawl and agro-industrial complex of today's Everglades. Instead, it considers a rural Everglades that has been overshadowed by the landscape's rapid social and environmental change. The stories gladesmen tell unfold in my mind in the black-and-white starkness of a Walker Evans photograph. Like Evans's images of 1930s Appalachia, gladesmen stories recall a past history that seems urgently close to us in time and utterly incomprehensible as an experience. Those who contributed to this ethnography are second- and third-generation gladesmen whose parents and grandparents settled in the region beginning in the mid-1800s. As the following chapters make clear, this book examines both this community's landscape emplacements and their displacements. Events detailed in the following chapters, such as the criminalization of alligator hunting or the founding of various protected areas, decisively altered gladeland subsistence strategies. At the same time, these events must be understood as indicators of the larger social and economic transformations taking place in southern Florida. Within a relatively brief period, about seventy-five years, southern Florida shifted from a largely rural, agrarian, and undeveloped landscape to one of the largest urban centers in the United States. Simply put, today very little possibility exists of making a living the Everglades way.

It is with misgivings that I use the term "gladesmen" in this book to describe this rural community of white settlers. In the course of my research, I found a letter written by John S. Lamb to the manager of the Loxahatchee National Wildlife Refuge. Written in the 1970s, Lamb's letter describes the people, including himself, who lived in the southeastern Everglades prior to the refuge's establishment. Lamb uses the term "gladesmen" in this letter. For instance, he says:

> Three professional gladesmen were working the Refuge Area when we began frog hunting there. Edgar Sorenson, a truly amazing woodsman . . . entered the Glades at the age of fifteen and spent the rest of his life there. He really was the Paul Bunyan of the Glades. He harvested whatever commodity [was] produced by the Glades which returned the price at the time, whether it be otter pelts, gator skins, frog legs, or moonshine whiskey![43]

The term "gladesmen" was not commonly used by locals, aside from Lamb, or by the various authors who employed locals to act as their guides during surveying or scientific research. Other terms, such as "glades hunters" or "crackers," appear more often in these texts.[44] I was drawn to Lamb's term, as it suggests the unbreakable ties these people had to the landscape itself and the rich associated Everglades culture that these ties entangle. Ben Orlove, in his evocative ethnography of highland Peruvian fishing communities, discusses his struggle to choose a term to describe the "persons-who-fished" at Lake Titicaca.[45] Orlove ultimately chose the term "fisherman" because fishing, as a discrete activity (going out on the boat and so on), appears to be a strictly male activity on Lake Titicaca. As a feminist scholar, I am very sensitive to the power of gendered language to obscure women's roles and economic contributions and, more seriously, to maintain social inequalities. So, like Orlove, I struggled with the process of naming. At various stages in writing this book I have used the term "gladesfolk" and "gladespeople." Also, like Orlove, I found such terms fairly awkward.

In the gladeland communities I am writing about, the household certainly served as the unit of production. For the most part, women's roles within the household, particularly the care of small children, prevented them from spending weeks in the backcountry. There are exceptions, though. During an interview, I asked H. Pete Whidden, of the Corkscrew settlement, if his mother had ever hunted with his father. He replied, "Yeah, she'd go 'gator hunting with him. . . . Me and my older brother, we went to school, and she would go in the woods, would trap, 'gator hunt." He then told me a story of his mother accidentally shooting his father while alligator hunting: "They was 'gator hunting, and the 'gator come up and he was on the other side over there. . . . She had a twenty gauge and she shot the 'gator and the buckshot glanced off and hit my dad. Well, it didn't even [hurt him], it just went under the skin." Whidden's story is the kind of the story that gets passed down within families, one of those tales that families tell to illustrate their own history — and to get a chuckle from guests. Alligator hunting figures throughout the Whidden family history, with wives, mothers, sisters, and children woven throughout their biographies of the landscape.

Yet as in the case of the fishermen on Lake Titicaca, very few women participated in backcountry hunting. When they did participate, it was generally by accompanying male relatives on trips into the backcountry. I ultimately chose the term "gladesmen" to acknowledge the ways hunting, as a set of material and semiotic practices, contributes to what it means to be a male within these communities. Masculinity as a subjectivity comes into being in the swamps. Being a man, like being human, is historically situated and contingent. Gladesmen subjectivity emerges through muddy, smoky, bloody relations with other animals, such as alligators; through particular objects, like guns and boats; and through tactile engagements (body memories?) in an often physically taxing environment, all bound to modernity's broader myths of sexual difference.

In using the term "gladesmen," I recognize that women's roles in the process of production and reproduction remain hidden. This is why I would like to make the distinction between the practice of hunting, which was typically done by men alone in the backcountry, and hunting as a larger economic activity. Hunting as a practice took place away from the household, away from the daily struggles of getting children off to school and scraping together meals during hard times. No doubt this was part of hunting's appeal. The hunter's landscape is a man's world, a world of hard labor, sweat, cigarette smoke, and raunchy jokes. The hunter's landscape is also one that features the displacement of women.

Those who participated in this research recall a period of time that is at least forty years distant. In all likelihood, this is the last generation of people who personally remember the Everglades as it was before the Army Corps of Engineers dramatically accelerated the drainage process in the 1940s. Glades families once lived all along the margins of the interior Everglades as well as on the small coastal islands ringing the western and southwestern coast. Except in areas that were once farmed, the traces of these communities are no longer discernable because of years of hurricane winds, fast-growing tropical vegetation, and the establishment of vast areas of protected wilderness. In other locations, wealthy communities (such as Marco Island and Naples), shopping malls, and the other signs of southern Florida's rapid development have replaced the shacks and small homesteads where glades families once lived. But this history—of former juke joints, backcountry camps, moonshine stills, and the like—continues to haunt the landscape like the burning swamp gases locals called ghost fires.

The Queen of the Everglades

We never liked that business of the King and the Queen of the Everglades. About ninety-nine percent of what they wrote about John
and Aunt Laura was pure fiction. Aunt Laura was a kind generous
Christian woman.

—NORMAN PADGETT, in J. T. Huffstodt,
Everglades Lawmen: True Stories of Game Wardens in the Glades

In pulp fiction, a narrative form that at times resembles ethnography, Laura
Upthegrove would have been called "low-rent" or, more charitably, a "bad
apple." Her story unfolds, as we will see in this book, along a tragic trajectory,
until it ends in a small-town grocery store located along the eastern shore of
Florida's Lake Okeechobee. Even these skeletal facts may be disputed. Com-
peting efforts to exaggerate and efface the particulars of her life have produced an untidy assemblage of partial truths. Upthegrove's notorious love
affair with an infamous outlaw led her family to distance themselves from
her memory, while this same notoriety inflamed the press's contradictory
accounts of her life and death. Some say that it was a "fit of temper," spurred
by a disagreement with a customer, that led her to grab a bottle of Lysol
off the shelf and drink it down that evening in 1927. If it was Lysol, a fa-
vored suicide method in the 1920s, her death would not have been easy. The
cresol-containing disinfectant would have burned her throat, corroded her
stomach, and eventually caused vascular collapse. Other troubles plagued
her besides a conflict over the correct change on an illegal liquor sale.

The legends about Laura Upthegrove are numerous. During the 1920s,
she was a member of the Ashley Gang,[1] a group of outlaws who robbed banks,
killed policemen, made and sold illegal liquor, and hijacked rum-runners on

the Gulf of Mexico. Most notably, the gang evaded capture for years. They taunted the police at every turn, dodged several posses, and repeatedly escaped from jail or prison. Their successful evasion of the law, at least until their leader's demise during a shoot-out one dark evening on a lonely bridge, was due, in part, to their intimate knowledge of the Everglades backcountry. Most of the gang's members had grown up in the Everglades, and during their time, they returned to camps hidden there. Almost a century later, the Ashley Gang remains a palpable figure in the mythology of the Everglades.

More personally, I must admit that the commonality of our first names has spurred my obsession-bordering fascination with Laura Upthegrove. Instead of downplaying this coincidence, I have chosen to treat this commonality as a research directive. Walter Benjamin compared his method of writing critical history to a sea journey on which the ship has been drawn off course by the magnetic North Pole. For Benjamin, critical illumination appears as we follow the deviations of history's main line. As he says, "Discover *that* North Pole."[2] Laura Upthegrove is this book's North Pole. We return to her story again and again. In doing so, we see how the past and the present, myth and memory, the human and nonhuman become entangled in the Everglades swamps and the swamps' rural communities.

Of course, names, the process of naming, and the gradual unraveling of a name's genealogy are endeavors fraught with powerful complications. This was certainly the case with the other Laura. She was called Laura Upthegrove and Laura Upthegrove-Tillman, and stories exist of her unlikely marriage to her half brother (endlessly repeated in newspaper accounts over the past several decades) that would have made her, finally, Laura Tracey. Her multiple proper names reveal something of her messy personal life and the formal political economy of kinship. Yet her association with the Everglades landscape slips away from these names, residing instead in her outlaw image and love affair with an Everglades gangster named John Ashley. For this association, the press referred to her as the "Queen of the Everglades."

2. LANDSCAPE ETHNOGRAPHY AND THE POLITICS OF NATURE

> Exploration is not so much a covering of surface distance as a study
> in depth: a fleeting episode, a fragment of landscape or a remark
> overheard may provide the only means of understanding and inter-
> preting areas which would otherwise remain barren of meaning.
> —CLAUDE LÉVI-STRAUSS, *Tristes Tropiques*

The Bill Ashley Jungles is a remembered landscape. Glades hunters named the Bill Ashley Jungles after a band of outlaws who hid out in the Everglades during the 1920s. Although there is an actual mangrove swamp within Everglades National Park that corresponds to the mangrove swamp old-timers used to call the Bill Ashley Jungles, it has been over fifty years since that name was part of an active landscape vernacular. Moreover, mangrove landscapes are terribly mobile, and so the mangrove swamp once known as the Bill Ashley Jungles has transformed itself many times in those fifty years. Nor does the name appear on contemporary Park Service maps — or on old maps, for that matter, since glades hunters were not mapmakers. This is a book about searching for the Bill Ashley Jungles and remembering as a critical practice.

The glades hunters I interviewed for this book were in their eighties and nineties when we worked together. They are the last generation for which the Bill Ashley Jungles was a lived experience, and several of those I interviewed have since passed away. There is nostalgia in their remembering — for instance, a nostalgia for a time when their claims to the landscape were not blocked by various constraints (of age, of access, and so many others). In other words, they yearn for an Everglades that is reimagined through the

Rhizophora mangle in the Bill Ashley
Jungles. Photograph by author.

lens of loss. We might understand nostalgia as the present's interventions into memory. But here we should not be overly concerned with articulating "the way it really was" or parsing the truth of memory and history.[1] Instead, we should look to what the tensions these practices of remembrance produce. Critically remembering the Bill Ashley Jungles entails allowing the past (selective, nostalgic, archetypal) to counter the cheap romance in the endless representations of the Everglades as a landscape of outlaws and outsiders. What we gain is a glimpse into an Everglades where the human, alligator, and mangrove worlds are hopelessly entangled and blurred, a landscape of local mythologies, economic struggles, and asymmetrical relations.

In this book, remembering as a critical practice should not be confused with critique. Critique is a process of breaking things down. We use ideas, often from critical theory, as the tools to help us emancipate the truths about the power dynamics of the world — the truths about the politics of meaning, structural inequalities, race, class and gender hegemonies, the fluidity of categories of difference, and so many more worthy targets. Yet in the quest for revelation through breaking down, the joy of invention, experimentation, and play often gets lost. Instead of using ideas to break things down (reduction), I am interested in using ideas to build things up (production). What gets produced, in this book at least, are maps of the remembered landscape. But these maps are not cartographies of "the way it really was." On the contrary, these maps will only help us get a bit less lost.

I refer to the gladesmen's Everglades as a "hunter's landscape." The hunter's landscape is a set of relations among humans and nonhumans that were shaped, in part, by the cultural practices and economic incentives of rural hunting in southern Florida. The hunter's landscape did not exist in isolation. Instead, as I show throughout this book, the hunter's landscape is entangled by a variety of agents who make their own territorial claims on the landscape. The Everglades, as we know it, has always been entangled at the intersection of the human and nonhuman worlds. In fact, we are only now beginning to understand how the Everglades of today is a result of the transformative work of mound-building prehistoric peoples and thousands of years of water flow and habitat formation. Certainly, we would be hard-pressed to locate any aspect of the contemporary Everglades, with its highly technical water management regimes and related land-use changes, that is pure nature. At the same time, the nonhuman Everglades has its own logic and rules of engagement that exist within these larger articulations of the human world, encompassing the flow of nutrients through marshes, the lifeworlds of animals and plants, algae, and the like. In the hunter's landscape, the milieus of the human and nonhuman worlds make claims on each other, as this book maps out, forming shifting assemblages and alliances.

Over the last several decades, cultural geographers and anthropologists have offered several approaches to theorizing the often hidden humanity of landscapes. Much of this work has focused on the ways in which natural-ized environments reverberate with cultural significance, acting as reposi-tories of cultural memory, false memories, mythology, and social identity and as sites of production and reproduction. Landscapes seem to "gather," to borrow Edward Casey's term, memories of childhood trips to the shore, Pintupi dreaming, Apache wisdom, perceptions of security and isolation, and vernacular acts of speaking, naming, and listening.[2] In a similar sense, other scholarship has interrogated the intersections of global conservation discourses, ecological claims, and proprietorships and the impact of these processes on local populations and livelihoods.[3]

In general, what these approaches share is an attention to the local, or localized, embodied, experience of landscape as well as a concern for how local landscape practices intersect with various constellations of power.[4] In doing so, this scholarship has focused attention on the social constructions and cultural relativism of spatial experiences. These approaches, and related work on space and place, have decidedly transformed our understanding of the significance of landscapes to peoples around the world — as sites of con-test, accord, and practice. Here, landscapes are always revising and are sub-ject to debate. They are conceptualized as a process by which subjectivities are formed and forming, a verb rather than a noun.[5] This rich and varied scholarship has moved us far beyond treating landscape as a "framing con-vention," as Eric Hirsch described the role of landscape within traditional ethnographic writing.[6]

Still, even as we have moved beyond treating landscape as a backdrop to culture, there remains an unproblematic sense of landscape as seden-tary and emplaced, with its nonhuman elements and processes consigned to conceptual spaces external to human life. In his lovely book *Landscape and*

Memory, Simon Schama argues that landscapes reflect a buildup of memory, history, and experience that is as compositional to landscapes as are layers of rock.[7] Indeed, the stories gladesmen tell, like those of the Bill Ashley Jungles, seem embedded within the very geography of swamp and hammock, like bits of poetry granting the landscape form. Yet the geographic metaphor is not quite apt. Considering history and memory as compositional strata continues to subtly externalize peoples and cultural practices from nature.

Landscapes may "mean" different things to various individuals and communities and, in turn, may be practiced in various ways. But what of the curious and unexpected connections that link and transform geography, people, animals, plants, and inorganic matters? Questions begging to be answered: How do animals speak to humans? How do hunters become animal? Where are the sites where the past becomes the present and the present stands still? Are rocks, water, and plants both real and enfabled? Do they have agency? Certainly these are questions that anthropologists comfortably pose in non-Western contexts.[8] Yet, as Bruno Latour has so eloquently argued, we less comfortably produce "symmetrical anthropologies" of hybridized nature–culture within contexts of Western modernity.[9]

I am using the term "landscape ethnography" to signal an approach to writing culture that is attentive to the ways in which *our relations with nonhumans produce what it means to be human.* Becoming human, becoming alligator, becoming mangrove, and so forth are contingent processes. They are also processes specific to particular temporalities, power relations, and geographies (material and imaginary). Donna Haraway calls the entities of these relations of becoming "companion species."[10] World making is the result of companionships among species, and this awareness, I believe Haraway is telling us, requires not a post-human ethnography but an ethnographic practice that is accountable to the *asymmetrical* relations of our collective lives. Landscapes—whether swamps or cities or rural farmlands—are assemblages of collective species, the products of collective desires and the asymmetrical relations among humans and nonhumans. This does not mean that the nonhuman world is without power. For instance, Paul Robbins convincingly shows how our beloved turfgrass monoculture produces "lawn people" as a kind of subjectivity, even though this dominant land cover is itself the product of a vast petro-chemical-industrial economic machine.[11]

Landscape ethnography, as I imagine it, is a practice of reintroducing and reinscribing the human back into the multispecies collective while at the same time being attuned to the politics of asymmetrical relations.

MANGROVE LOGIC

A few ideas from the work of Gilles Deleuze and Félix Guattari, particularly their notion of the *rhizome,* have shaped my approach to research and writing about the hunter's landscape. Deleuze and Guattari's spatial philosophy offers a way of theorizing landscapes as complex and changing assemblages of relations that dissolve and displace the boundaries of nature and culture. Instead of seeing place or landscape as sites that beckon, contain, and are transformed by the human world, Deleuze and Guattari insist that the world's properties (material, semiotic, human, and nonhuman) come into being only through their relations.[12] There is no finality to these relations of becoming. Instead there are only temporary sites of assemblage. For Deleuze and Guattari, the rhizome is a metaphor for the unreasonable logics of these world-making processes *as well as* a kind of heuristic for producing philosophy (research and writing). The rhizome as a world logic and a writing machine is critical to this book's construction, as I show in the rest of this chapter.

It may sound like magical thinking, but the Bill Ashley Jungles led me to this rhizome approach. As I describe below, the mangrove swamps that figure throughout this book are inescapably Deleuze-Guattarian. My exploration of these swamps—scrambling through their tangled masses, writing about their connections—left me feeling as if I had little choice but to use Deleuze and Guattari's work as a compass. My own sense of how we create theory, or put concepts to work, has been guided by an overriding interest in exploring the chance ways in which ideas speak to each other. To spend time in the Bill Ashley Jungles is to encounter the rhizome at work.

The most prominent species in the Bill Ashley Jungles is the red mangrove, or *Rhizophora mangle. R. mangle* grows in dense and impenetrable thickets, making the Bill Ashley Jungles a landscape of rhizomic excess. The entangled habitats of mangroves are referred to as "mangals," almost a tautology, as the biologist Peter Hogarth notes.[13] The trees' aerial and stilting prop roots emerge from their trunks (as well as from other roots), forming an impassable jumble of limbs, leaves, roots, and trunks. Mile after mile of mangrove swamps form a porous boundary demarcating the freshwater Everglades from the salty waters of the bays and Gulf of Mexico beyond. Although porous, these swamps also buffer the Everglades interior from the damaging winds and tides of periodic hurricanes. In the mangroves, fresh- and saltwater mingle; sediments gather and flow. The boundaries of mangrove swamps are always shifting. At the same time, these swamps are foundational to the life cycles of fish, birds, and other animals. Below the water, mangrove root systems serve as "nurseries" for many species of fish that live their adult lives in the reefs beyond. Above in the mangrove treetops, wading birds and pelicans nest; their presence leaves the mangrove's brilliant green canopy coated with broad spatters of white guano. Mangrove swamps, such as the Bill Ashley Jungles, are both in-between and becoming. They are sites of movement, production, and heterogeneous connections.

Deleuze and Guattari's rhizome helps me think through the complexities of world making that takes place in the Bill Ashley Jungles. Here is a place of multispecies becoming. Hunters become hunters through their connection with alligators — they sound like alligators, think like alligators, and immerse themselves in alligator blood and flesh. Here is a place of confusing, nonlinear networks. Mangrove tunnels provide passage through these swamps, until the passageways close up and reform elsewhere. Here is a place of shifting registers, where the imaginary, semiotic, material, and economic assemble to generate territory and territorial claims. Enormous, fantastic snakes keep city people, often the same ones who buy luxury leather products made from the skin of alligators, from entering the Bill Ashley Jungles.

The rhizome also helps me think about ethnographic writing. Scientists first exploring the southern Everglades found the region's mangrove swamps unsettlingly inscrutable.[14] Missing is the order of a northeastern forest. Instead, scientists describe these swamps as "mazes" and "labyrinths." In its liberating rhizomeness, the mangrove is both tree and antitree. For Deleuze and Guattari, rhizomes resist tree logic, or "arbolescence." The goal of tree logic is descriptive and reductive, a practice of tracing and replicating what already lurks "in the dark recesses of memory and language."[15]

A key characterization of the rhizome is that it is a *map*, not a tracing. Maps, unlike tracings, allow for multiple "entryways" and practices of modification, as do the labyrinthine mangrove swamps. Maps always offer the possibility of new routes, new configurations, and new horizons. The difference between a map and a tracing, according to Deleuze and Guattari, is that the map "is entirely oriented toward an experimentation in contact with the real."[16] Therefore, the rhizome is not only a metaphor for thinking through the world's relations, or in this case, theorizing the Everglades landscape, but also a *model for producing landscape ethnography*. Make a map, not a tracing.

MAKE A MAP, NOT A TRACING

This book should be read as a part of the Everglades entanglement, or better, as an experiment with the rhizome's logic. For Deleuze and Guattari, the rhizome is an endless array of connection and alliance. As they suggest, "The tree imposes the verb 'to be,' but the fabric of the rhizome is the conjunction ,'and . . . and . . . and.'"[17] Writing a rhizome of multiplying conjunction upends and problematizes academic conventions and expectations of narrative, not to mention the inherent limitations of a book. Books cannot be endless and multiple. Within these limitations, I have allowed the rhizome to guide this book's composition. Each chapter maps the course of a particular trajectory within the Everglades rhizome. I have treated this mapping as an experiment (expedition) of discovery, allowing the unexpected and curious connections and dissidences encountered along the way to remain. Instead of asking, What does this mean? I ask, Where does this go? In this spirit, I have resisted those ingrained urges to efface findings (by which I mean connections encountered along the way) that appear obscure and resistant to the standard logics of academic argumentation.

In this book several themes emerge. First, the hunter's landscape is ripe with tactics of territoriality (or ways of ordering the landscape to stake and maintain claims of various natures). For instance, in chapter 3, which details the practices of Everglades alligator hunting, several recurring refrains order the territory of the hunter's landscape. For Delueze and Guattari, refrains are repetitions (almost like tropes) within an assemblage that designate territory. In the hunter's landscape these refrains include earth, fire, and flesh. Animals and humans emerge as collaborative agents of territory within these refrains, with animals (particularly alligators) shaping the territorial practices of hunters and hunters shaping the territorial practices of alligators. In chapter 6, we see how gladesmen claim hunting territories and enforce those claims through various practices of intimidation. Often these practices of territoriality are subtler: fantastic snakes mark territory, mangroves produce territory (even as hunters beat the mangroves back), past events become emplaced and define territory (the Bill Ashley Jungles, for example), and so on.

Second, the hunter's landscape has its own temporal rhythms. Time is marked not by hour and day but, instead, by seasonal change. The region's rainy and dry seasons radically reconfigure the landscape, and in doing so they reorganize the alliances and practices of people, animals, and plant life. Throughout this book, we see the hunter's landscape shift about in accord with seasonal fluctuations of available water, heat, and fire. Yet time also unfolds (and refolds upon itself) through various movements. Rhizomes disrupt the linear progress of time, or at least our understanding of time. A rhizome has "neither beginning nor end, but always a middle *(milieu)* from which it grows and which it overspills."[18] We may think of rhizomes as roots that grow in time, with that growth a testament to the progress of time. But the rhizome's new shoots entangle the old, forming new knotty formations. This is how the past (partially remembered) and the present come together in the Bill Ashley Jungles.

Chapter 4 of this book, entitled "The Travels of Snakes, Mangroves, and Men," explores the travels of hunters through the backcountry, their timeless meandering across vast prairies and their slow-going transects of the mangrove jungles. Yet it is not only humans that are mobile. Indeed, the Everglades landscape is also in constant motion, as are the creatures, nutrients, charged particles, and plant life that are humans' fellow travelers. Although time in the hunter's landscape emerges through movement (nonlinear and syncopated), time is also practiced as a mixed-up past–present dialectic.

Third, a broad politics of nature constrains the rhizome's liberties. In the Bill Ashley Jungles, humans exert an enormous power over the landscape's formation and transformations, as I discuss below. But it is not only humans who have the power of governance in the Bill Ashley Jungles. Mangroves, fire, alligators, snakes, and many other objects are critical to the processes of world making (and subject making). More importantly, many of the powerful agents of change in the Bill Ashley Jungles — as is the case everywhere — are hybrid socionatural processes. For example, rising sea levels have and will continue to have a profound power to reshape the Bill Ashley Jungles. Once I spent hours with Glen Simmons and my father looking for a site Glen had used as a camp fifty years earlier on the Joe River. This is a labyrinthine landscape, made up of thousands of small mangrove islands and twisting creeks. As Glen grew increasingly frustrated, I thought that maybe his memory was playing tricks on him — though Glen's memory of landscape features after decades was always stunningly accurate. Finally we stopped the boat to explore on foot. There, where he thought it should be, were the decaying trunks of some cabbage palms that had once marked the site of his old camp. Now the salt water covered this spot of once dry land, killing the palms and allowing mangroves to grow thick at the site. Glen firmly believed that the sea level is rising, and sea level rise is the perfect example of a powerful socionatural process. In this book, I pay close attention to the ways the nonhuman world exerts its power over the hunter's landscape. Latour has defined politics as "the entire set of tasks that allow the progressive composition of a common world."[19] Human, nonhuman, and hybrid processes govern this progressive world making. It is this collective power of composition that I refer to when I talk about the politics of nature.

State-sponsored development schemes have had an enormous impact on the hunter's landscape. In their work, Deleuze and Guattari particularly focus on the state as a "megamachine" of capture.[20] Through the processes of capture, as Mark Bonta and John Proveti describe in their excellent companion to Deleuze and Guattari's *A Thousand Plateaus,* the state overcodes preexisting assemblages of humans and nonhumans. The state apparatus acts as "an organizing, centralizing, hierarchizing machine" that transforms "activity into work (labor), territories into 'the land,' and surplus value into capital."[21] But states, like the cultures and places they seek to engineer, are hardly monolithic entities.[22] Instead, modern states control resources and peoples through a profoundly complex architecture of administrative agencies, quasi-governmental organizations, and a variety of nested and overlapping private–public "partnerships." These are assemblages rife with political contest, having their own cultures, histories, and terrains of expertise to defend and stake out. Throughout this book, I have treated the "state" as a heterogeneous composition of agencies and actors, loosely bound by a broader and changing vision of the Everglades, deploying specific state-sponsored apparatuses of capture. These apparatuses of capture (water supply and drainage practices, natural resource management, Everglades restoration activities) have profoundly altered the Everglades, constraining the actions of men, plants, water, and nonhuman animals within the landscape.

Certainly, one of the ways states exercise power is by setting bureaucratic, legal, and discursive boundaries on various ways of thinking about and acting on nature, often calling on scientific or technical knowledge to defend these restrictions.[23] Andrew Pickering, in his exploration of scientific practice and production, puts the mangle to work in ways that nicely overlay Deleuze and Guattari's project, and he illustrates the boundary keeping that takes place within territorial assemblages. For Pickering, scientific practice emerges out of a machine-like interplay of material and social agency along with processes that create both resistance and accommodation to the business of scientific practice. This mangle that is scientific practice also recalls, for Pickering, the laundry press of the same name used to "squeeze water out of the washing."[24] In the hunter's landscape, scientific production becomes an apparatus of capture that transforms the practices of rural families within the landscape, as I identify in chapter 5, "Searching for Paradise in the Florida Everglades." I show there how creating the Everglades as a landscape of ecological worth is contingent upon the collaborations of local glades guides and visiting naturalists. Early field surveys and expeditions into the Everglades backcountry would not have been possible without those collaborations. Yet, as I show, the ascendancy of the scientific value of the Everglades sets in motion related processes that result in the banishment of the local families from the landscape itself. In other words, local guides unknowingly participate in their own entrapment.

In chapter 6, "Alligator Conservation, Commodities, and Tactics of Subversion," I track the ways state-sponsored alligator management programs, promoted and enforced by the Florida Department of Game and Fresh Water

Fish, emerge as another critical constraint on the relationships among hunters, animals, and their practices of territoriality. For decades, these regulatory frameworks and shifting modes of enforcement drove alligator hunting underground, criminalizing a time-honored economic strategy and transforming hunters into poachers. Yet even in the context of capture, Deleuze and Guattari's rhizome offers avenues of escape (or ways of thinking around the binaries of structure and agency). In their celebration of Franz Kafka's work, for instance, Deleuze and Guattari treat Kafka's work as an experimental machine that derails social domination, a minor literature whose liberating politics is "neither imaginary or symbolic."[25] Like a minor language, glades hunters create escape routes from the capture that is the legislation, game wardens, and penalties that make alligator hunting illegal in southern Florida. They do so by transforming the Everglades into a "landscape of subversion," a reconfigured territorial assemblage.

In sum, the central premise of this book is that landscapes are assemblages constituted by humans and nonhumans, material and semiotic processes, histories both real and partially remembered. Moreover, these diverse properties form an assemblage characterized by rhizomic heterogeneity and interconnections. Even so, a broader politics of nature works to constrain the entanglement's freedom of movement and connectivity. In some locations this apparatus of capture succeeds; in other sites the rhizome's tendencies toward evasion and reformation counter these constraints. This book does not attempt to disarticulate the assemblage's entanglements. Instead, it attempts to map the hunter's landscape, particularly focusing in on the territorial practices of hunters and animals. This book should be read as an experiment with Deleuze and Guattari's spatial philosophy and as an experiment in writing the rhizomic landscape that is the Everglades.

The Notorious Ashley Gang

> A rhizome has no beginning or end; it is always in the middle,
> between things, interbeing, *intermezzo.*
>
> —GILLES DELEUZE and FÉLIX GUATTARI, *Kafka: Toward a Minor Literature*

For such a notorious figure, John Ashley was slightly built. In one photograph, he countenances a rakish vulnerability, a quality Laura Upthegrove must have found attractive. Though he stares coolly into the camera, he looks uneasy in his suit. Perhaps the suit is borrowed. Certainly, the sleeves are hemmed too high, exposing his delicate wrists. His black eye patch, with its strap disappearing into his dark pomaded hair, contrasts sharply with his all-white suit. Yet the symbolism at play in this black-and-white color scheme is too easy. Perhaps the photograph's most significant incongruity is that Ashley is wearing the suit in the first place, as he was hardly raised to wear such clothing.

By profession, Joe Ashley, John's father, was a woodchopper for Henry Flagler's Florida East Coast Railway. Flagler's railway reached West Palm Beach, in southern Florida, in 1894. Encouraged by persistent lobbying and a significant land contribution by Julia Tuttle, Miami's matriarch, Flagler eventually extended the railway southward to Miami and then, in a mammoth feat of engineering, over the sea to Key West. This railway was a critical artery in the tycoon's Florida empire, an effort he began after retiring from Standard Oil, which he had cofounded. Aside from the railway, Flagler's interests included several lavish resort hotels, such as the Breakers in Palm Beach, and an agricultural and real estate development company. Along the way he financed the construction of schools, hospitals, and churches. These

John Ashley *(right)* with unidentified bystander. Photograph courtesy of the Fort Lauderdale Historical Society.

unparalleled capital investments were key to southern Florida's transformation from a dismal, swampy outpost to a Gilded Age playground.

As do all empires, Flagler's required an enormous input of cheap labor. The Ashley family, like thousands of other families, became anonymous contributors to empire and thus to the transformation of the Everglades. Joe Ashley, his wife Lugenia, and their nine children moved from Fort Myers to the Pompano Beach area in 1904. Several years later the family relocated to West Palm Beach. Throughout this period, Joe and his elder sons cut wood that was used to power the railway's steam engines. As was typical for Everglades settlers, the Ashley family supplemented their wage earnings by hunting, fishing, and raising vegetables. At some point, Joe Ashley began to operate a whiskey still and sell illegal liquor, an enterprise that would become a family business.

The younger boys, including John Ashley, spent their time hunting and trapping in the woods of southeastern Florida. By age eleven, John's shooting accuracy was said to rival his father's.[1] Edmond Rodgers, a family friend and father-in-law to William "Bill" Ashley, the oldest son, described John as the bravest and coolest man he had ever known. John's shooting skill was legendary. As Rodgers recalled, "I believe he was the best shot with a rifle or a revolver that I ever saw. . . . I have seen him ride along in a wagon, take his revolver and shoot off the head of a quail, off-handed twenty to thirty yards."[2] Like many hardscrabble Florida families engaged in empire building, the Ashleys got along by skirting the law at times, in relatively minor offenses such as hunting out of season or selling moonshine. John Ashley's murder of DeSoto Tiger tipped the scales.

DeSoto Tiger was the son of Mary Tiger and Tom Tiger, a well-regarded Seminole leader. In the early 1980s, Ada Coats Williams interviewed Frank Shore, DeSoto Tiger's brother-in-law.[3] According to Shore, and substantiated by other accounts, John Ashley joined a group of Seminole hunters in December 1911. The hunters had invited Ashley into their camp because they were friends of John's brother Bill. From this camp in the glades outside Fort Lauderdale, the group hunted alligators and trapped otter. Though otter hides were selling well that season, going for around a dollar each, the group decided to break camp and return home for Christmas. Apparently,

DeSoto Tiger was anxious to see his wife, Ada Micco, and their newborn daughter, Flora.

The project of empire intervenes at this point in the story as well. According to Shore, the Seminole hunters were good friends with a dredge operator named Captain Fowry who was working on the North New River Canal project. It took nearly six years to build the canal, which ultimately linked Lake Okeechobee to the Atlantic Ocean at Fort Lauderdale. The North New River Canal project was the first of several canal projects initiated by the Everglades Drainage District, a massive state-sponsored swampland reclamation effort designed to spur agricultural development. Shore said that DeSoto's group trusted Fowry to such an extent that the dredgeman would store the hunters' stockpile of hides until they were ready to sell them. So on the early morning of the day the hunters were to return home, DeSoto Tiger filled his dugout canoe with the party's accumulated hides and prepared to take them to Fowry. As he poled his dugout canoe from camp, Ashley asked Tiger if he could go with him, saying he wanted to buy some supplies from Fowry. Ashley then climbed into Tiger's dugout carrying his Winchester rifle. They never arrived at Fowry's.

Concerned over Tiger's disappearance, his relatives and others sailed their canoes to Fort Lauderdale, the location of the closest trading post. There they learned that Ashley had taken a train to Miami. Tiger's family then poled their canoes southward, through the rivers of the Everglades, until they reached Biscayne Bay and Miami. An account published in the *Seminole Tribune* describes the surprise of the tourists assembled at the Royal Palm Hotel, one of Flagler's gems, at the sight of Tiger's search party sailing past in their canoes. After docking their canoes, they soon found that Ashley had already come and gone, selling the otter hides for $1,200 at the Girtman Brothers Trading Post.[4] Several days later, a suction dredge boat brought Tiger's body up from the canal.

By the mid-1920s, almost the entire Ashley family would become collaborators in and casualties of John Ashley's violent and bloody rampage across the Everglades. Still, years later, community members recalled the family's hospitality. For instance, Oren B. "O. B." Padgett, who once dated one of John Ashley's cousins and later became a deputy sheriff of Palm Beach

County, described the Ashleys as "very, very friendly people who always welcomed you when you were a guest in their home."[5] Edmond Rodgers echoed this sentiment, saying, "With all truthfulness . . . I have never seen a more generous and open, big-hearted family of people in my life, always ready to help those who were in need, or in distress, and feed the hungry; that was the Ashleys, those desperate people of who you have heard so much and of whom John was one."[6]

3. EARTH, FIRE, AND FLESH
Territorial Refrains

> To become animal is to participate in movement, to stake out the
> path of escape in all its positivity, to cross a threshold, to reach a
> continuum of intensities that are valuable only in themselves, to find
> a world of pure intensities where all forms come undone.
>
> —DELEUZE and GUATTARI, *Kafka: Toward a Minor Literature*

Several years ago I was walking with Glen Simmons, then in his late
eighties, down a weedy section of the Old Ingraham Highway, a remnant
road within Everglades National Park that once served as a major thorough-
fare for backcountry hunters. The day was warm, that welcoming warmth of
a southern Florida winter afternoon, and the surrounding marsh was alive
with the sounds of flitting warblers, herons, and egrets. In parts of the glades
the dry winter parches the earth, and on that day the sweet musty aroma of
sun-baked algae mats filled the air. Throughout our slow walk, we bent to
examine the many alligator drag marks that crossed our path, sloppy inden-
tations where alligators had jerkily hoisted themselves across and over the
road's muddy banks. Together, he a bit unsteadily, we crouched down and
peered into these drag marks, looking for traces of claws and tail, trying to
guess the alligator's size and how long ago it had passed through.

Walking with Simmons, I imagined we were characters in a natural history detective story, putting together clues of past wildlife adventures. Then
he said something that abruptly dissolved this line of thought. I distinctly
remember that we were poking at some rather antique-looking alligator
scat, and I asked him, "When you see this, do you think of hunting?" At
the time, I was surprised that I asked him this question, the passing of years

American alligator.
Photograph by Deborah Mitchell.

having long erased his hunting days. He paused, and then slowly, with great deliberation, said, "Oh, yes." Though he said only these two words, his tone conveyed an urgent matter-of-factness. I realized then that we were experiencing vastly distinct Everglades and that his was and would always be a hunter's landscape.

Alligator hunting is often described as the "nastiest way to make a dollar," and the following descriptions certainly illustrate that sentiment. At the same time, alligator hunting was one of the most reliable sources of income for glades people, for alligators could be hunted year-round whereas other game animals were seasonal. Fur-bearing animals — raccoon, otter, or mink — were only valuable when their pelts were thick in the wintertime. Without a doubt, market demand shaped hunting practices. Changes in fashion (plumed hats, alligator purses, belts, and suitcases) and corresponding prices for these animal objects altered which animals hunters sought and how they prepared their skins and hides. For instance, the craze for raccoon-skin caps in the 1950s, instigated by Fess Parker's role in the Walt Disney television film *Davy Crockett: Indian Fighter* (1954), reignited the dormant raccoon-skin trade, with rural folks all over the country sending parcels of 'coons off to the Sears, Roebuck company.

Later in this book I discuss the politics and economics of alligator hunting, examining the market and regulatory frameworks that shaped the supply and demand of the trade. But before proceeding to those analyses, here I describe the practice of alligator hunting itself. At its most basic, the hunter's aesthetic is one of bloodshed and boredom. Though we often think of aesthetics as the conventions of taste, particularly as they relate to a refined contemplation of the beautiful, Susan Buck-Morss reminds us that originally the term "aesthetics" suggested a form of knowing involving "the whole corporeal sensorium."[1] Everglades hunters relied on their instincts, experience, and senses to track, kill, and prepare glades animals. The practice was graphic, messy, and physically taxing — an aesthetics of bodies, both animals and humans, immersed in water, mud, and smoke. In this chapter, my wish is to evoke some of the tactile immediacy of the hunter's landscape.

Like a song, the aesthetics of the hunter's landscape is composed of repeated refrains, akin to what Roland Barthes, in his *Lover's Discourse:*

Fragments, calls "figures."[2] Barthes offers a detailed and wide-ranging compendium of "figures" that characterize the experience of lovers. For Barthes, figures are those recognizable phrases, images, or the "read, heard, felt" of a particular social discourse, such as being in love.[3] Barthes's figures of love include *waiting by the phone, amorous declarations,* and *suffering from jealousy,* shared instances of experience we all recognize. Barthes maps love's figuration, and in doing so, he transforms what seems profoundly personal, being in love, to a familiar poetics of shared humanity. Yet Barthes's work does more than simply characterize the contours of love's landscape. When reading Barthes, we get a sense of the claims-making project of being in love, what Barthes refers to as the "will-to-possess."[4] All those shared glances and instances of finishing each other's sentences produce claims upon another, demarcating the territory of intimacy.

Deleuze and Guattari also are interested in the ways certain recognizable and repeated figures can create and demarcate territory. They use the term "refrain" to describe these blocks of content, defining a refrain as "*any aggregate of matters of expression that draws a territory and develops territorial motifs and landscapes.*"[5] Refrains take on many forms; they are sound, image, and gesture. Examples that Deleuze and Guattari give include certain birdsongs that establish boundaries within a forest or the encircling wall of sound formed by a television's blare. Although refrains come in many forms, they also mark different kinds of territory, including the lover's refrain that "territorializes the sexuality of the loved one,"[6] a point of convergence with Barthes.

If we use the rhizome to think through the material and semiotic processes that entangle the human and nonhuman worlds, then refrains are repeated figures within this entanglement. Bonta and Proveti, in their insightful book on Deleuze and Guattari, argue that a refrain "not only creates and holds the territory, but also becomes the motif or repeatable theme of a landscape."[7] Although the refrains of hunting are varied — from the smell of damp mangrove smoke to an earful of high-pitched mosquitoes — I am particularly interested in the "inventiveness," as Bruce Braun has so well described it, of the nonhuman world.[8] The refrains I explore in this chapter, *earth, fire,* and *alligator flesh,* are not static and fixed. Instead, they are shifting states, continually becoming and becoming undone; they are refrains of movement and transformation. These refrains suggest the world-making, human-making power of plants, mud, reptiles, and all the rest we used to call nature.

EARTH (LAND AND WATER)

The earth in the Florida Everglades takes many forms. It may be coated with algal mats that dry into cracked white blankets during the winter; it may be a mixture of warm water — salty, fresh, or brackish — with still sediment above and waist-deep mud below. In other areas the earth's surface is marked by protruding pinnacles of bare rock interspersed with deep crevasses that may be filled with water or rough vegetation. For Deleuze and Guattari, refrains mark different kinds of territory — geospatial, spiritual, emotional, disciplinary, and so on. Yet they also believe that all refrains, whether conceptual or material, have a kind of geospatial concomitant that ultimately refers to land ("a Natal, a Native"). A refrain, they say, "*always carries earth with it.*"[9] And the hunter's landscape is ever so earthy.

Alligators are animals both *of land* and *of water,* like the Everglades itself. Indeed, the refrains of the hunter's landscape revolve around the difficulties of dealing with animals and a landscape of amphibious ambiguities. Over the millennium, alligators have evolved in ways that make possible lives spent within this watery landscape. For instance, an alligator's circulatory system allows it to stay submerged for several hours at a time (depending on the water's temperature and the alligator's rate of activity). When an alligator is submerged, its blood bypasses its lungs and is routed directly to the heart. This versatility aids in oxygen conservation, for when an alligator is holding its breath, its lungs cannot provide fresh oxygen to the bloodstream.[10] Alligators also have highly specialized sense organs on their faces, called dome pressure receptors, which signal the slightest ripple in the water's surface, a helpful trait for an animal that often hunts in dark, murky waters.[11] As cold-blooded animals, alligators are very sensitive to fluctuations in seasonal temperatures, so sensitive, in fact, that when an alligator's body temperature drops below sixty degrees, its ability to digest food is compromised. Therefore, moving between water and land helps an alligator regulate its body temperature and survive the winter's winds and chilly waters.

In the water alligators are highly agile and fast. They can swim over one mile per hour and sustain much faster bursts of speed when hunting for food. To swim, they propel themselves forward with their tails, using a side-to-side motion; their webbed feet help guide their movement. Their tails are so powerful that they can use them to lift themselves up and across the water's surface, seemingly hydroplaning, as well as to lunge out of the water, propelling themselves up to five feet into the air. An alligator leaping vertically from the water is a trick that never fails to awe visitors viewing alligator-feeding shows at various Florida roadside attractions. Alligators are less graceful on land, tending to lumber about taking the path of least resistance. Often they pull themselves along preestablished "slides," or pathways in the mud, rather than walk upright over dry land. Yet no one should be complacent near an alligator on land. For short stretches, alligators can run at speeds averaging thirty miles per hour, though they can only run in straight lines and tire quickly. This land–water versatility allows alligators to claim territories in most of southern Florida's habitats — in the wet prairies; in ponds and lakes; in the mangrove jungles, the pinelands, and hammocks; and today, in the thousands of miles of canals that drain the landscape.

At its most basic, hunting is a territorial practice. Hunters claimed particular geographies within a landscape as their own, calling on community-recognized conventions to establish *who* was allowed to hunt *where.* When these customary conventions of territory failed, hunters employed a variety of tactics to discourage those who posed a threat to these territorial boundaries, as I detail in this book's sixth chapter. But more fundamentally, hunting entails an intervention into animal territories and territorial practices. Alligators are supremely territorial animals. Not only do alligators claim certain territories, but they create, maintain, and defend those territories. To pursue alligators successfully, hunters need to know how to locate alligators at different times of the year, across varying types of habitats within the Everglades landscape mosaic. The hunter's landscape, therefore, is composed of refrains that forge connections between the territorial practices of animals and the territorial practices of people. These connections, as Deleuze and Guattari would have it, are refrains of *reterritorialization.* In the hunter's landscape, the territorial practices of alligators, and other animals, are reconfigured into an assemblage of human–animal territoriality.

Unidentified man pulling an alligator from an Everglades "alligator hole," April 1906.
Photograph by Julian Dimock; printed by permission of the American Museum of Natural History.

In the Florida Everglades, hunters used two methods to hunt alligators, techniques that corresponded to differences in how alligators inhabit and create their territories during the rainy and dry seasons of the year. Hunters used the term "pole-hunting" to describe hunting alligators from their underground dens during the day and the term "fire-hunting" to describe hunting alligators at night in larger waterways. Generally, seasonal changes in Everglades water levels determined where alligators could be found. Pole-hunting from caves occurred during the dry winter months, when walking the marshes was possible and alligators could be readily located in their ponds and dens. Or as Pete Whidden told me, you pole-hunted when it was dry "'cause when it was wet, there ain't no telling, he [the alligator] might be at that cave, or he might be out yonder in the cypress. . . . No telling where he was at."

Not only do alligators inhabit these habitats, but they are also the architects of their territories. During the rainy summer months, alligators tend to roam for miles throughout the flooded Everglades marshes. Yet when the rains cease and the marshes begin to dry up, alligators congregate in any available pool of water, often returning year after year to the same "alligator hole." Alligators not only take up residence in these holes but also create them and keep them open as the dry season progresses. They do so by wallowing in the mud and sediment and by pushing the mud and vegetation around to form deeper depressions in the earth. As water levels drop in the Everglades, alligators continue to push mud and vegetation to the sides of the holes to maintain standing reservoirs of water. Though Everglades hunters knew the location of most alligator holes within their hunting territories, new alligator holes were easily detected. The banks of alligator holes stand out against the utter flatness of the surrounding glade plane, particularly in places where an alligator has piled the mud high. There is a lush richness to these ponds also clearly discernable from a distance. Alligator holes are immense reservoirs of biological productivity during the dry winter months, a point Frank Craighead Sr. detailed in one of the earliest discussions of alligator ecology.[12] While the rest of the land is parched, alligator holes are filled with fish, snails, and other small creatures that attract wading birds, turtles, snakes, otters, raccoons, and deer. Seemingly the entirety of the Everglades food chain becomes condensed within these muddy reservoirs of water.

For these reasons, alligator hunters could easily locate alligator holes and, during the winter months, be fairly certain to find at least one resident alligator. Yet actually retrieving the animal from one of these holes was tedious and difficult. Alligators are extremely sensitive to sound and movement, and as soon as an alligator senses the presence of something unusual, it will take refuge within its subterranean den. These dens, also called caves, are passages that lead several feet back into the earth from the banks of an alligator hole. Many times the bedrock around an alligator hole will be eroded or fractured, creating a labyrinthine network of tunnels that an alligator uses as refuge.[13] If these natural tunnels are not present, alligators will excavate the mud out along the side of the pond or dig below the roots of an over-hanging tree, creating their own earthly dens. Alligator dens may extend horizontally ten feet or more into the surrounding glade. Depending upon the availability of air within these caves, alligators can stay hidden within the earth for several days at a time.

To get at the alligator, secure and stubborn within its den, hunters needed to force the animal to emerge from the earth. Hence the hunter's refrain of earth, like most refrains, is one of staking a claim on the territory of an-other, in this case the alligator's territory. Yet the earth is hardly passive. In-stead, the earth's muddy ambiguities shape the relationship between hunters and alligators. The earth enfolds alligators in hidden subterranean territories, while at the same time, alligators reconfigure the earth by wallowing it out. Hunters wade and slog through the water, knee-deep in mud, each step an exercise in freeing oneself from the earth. Becoming human and becoming reptile is a becoming with mud.

Hunters, of course, were there to try and displace alligators from the earth so that they could remove and sell the animals' skins (mud enlivens the global hide market). To do so, alligator hunters spent a lot of time try-ing to agitate alligators, hoping to force the alligators to emerge from their caves. To reach these underground animals, hunters would insert an iron rod, a literal stake to forge this claim, through the roof of the alligator's den and poke and prod at the animal. These iron rods, called "gator rods" were long, often over six feet, and about three-eighths inch in diameter. Hunters walked across the glades, moving from one alligator hole to the next and using their gator rods to investigate each den they encountered along the way. As hunters knew most of the layout of existing alligator holes, since the animals tend to use the same holes year after year, hunters were also familiar with the direction and location of underground dens. If, upon approach, a hunter did not see an alligator lying along the hole's bank or in the water, he would start at the end of the den, or where he thought the den ended, and work toward the den's mouth, pushing the rod through the earth until he found the alligator. In many cases, a hunter's first contact with an alligator was a connection made through the earth.

Commonly, Everglades hunters used the term "pole-hunting" to refer to pursuing alligators from their underground dens. The term reflects a techno-

Pole-hunting in the Florida Everglades. One hunter probes the alligator's underground cave with a rod, while the other man waits to capture the animal with a noose. Photograph by Julian Dimock, Broad River, Everglades, 1906; printed by permission of the American Museum of Natural History.

logical evolution in hunting strategies, harkening back to a time before rifles were used for alligator hunting. Prior to the late nineteenth century, accurate rifles were not readily available. Instead, in this earlier era, hunters used a baited hook to drag alligators from their dens. Large hooks were attached to a sturdy cypress pole, hence the name "pole-hunting," and positioned just inside the opening to the alligator's den. Positioning the hook required one person to carefully wade into the alligator's pond and then ram the hooked pole into the alligator's den. When the alligator bit the hook, it took several men to drag it out of its den. After the alligator was brought out in the open waters of the pond, a task that involved considerable struggle, a member of the hunting party would sever the animal's spinal cord using an axe.

The availability of reliable rifles transformed the practice of alligator hunting in many ways. For generations, popular lore characterized alligator hides as simply impenetrable by bullets.[14] Bullets, it was said, merely glanced off the animal's hide, hardly slowing down the reptile's beastly progress. Like that of the great dragon Leviathan, an alligator's scaly armor was considered immune to man's glancing blows. The availability of more accurate rifles put an end to these popular notions. Glades hunters seemed to prefer the ever-popular .22 long rifle, whose bullets can easily penetrate an alligator's hide. These modern rifles allowed hunters to work the glades alone, or with one other partner, rather than in a group of several men hunting together. As a hunter working alone did not have to share income earned from hides with others, these newer guns made alligator hunting a much more practical and efficient form of labor.

Still, hunters had to be accurate shots. Although a bullet can certainly penetrate an alligator's hide, in doing so it damages the hide and makes it less marketable. To protect the valuable hide, glades hunters tried to shoot the animal in the head (which also ensured a quicker end as well). Bullets will ricochet off an alligator's tough skull. Therefore, hunters aimed for the soft spots, such as the alligator's eye or ear or the back of its skull where the bony cranium ends. The "trick," according to LeRoy Overstreet, who hunted alligators for over fifty years, was to "place the bullet so it would enter the soft spot and then travel on to the center of the spine or brain."[15] Waiting for that perfect shot required immeasurable patience, particularly since an alligator often will remain in its den for several hours, even against an arsenal of tricks intended to get it out. To ensure they were ready for the shot, hunters would place "a feeler inside the cave, a big stalk of sawgrass or a willow top," as Glen Simmons explained it to me. When they saw that feeler move, Simmons said, they would "pick up [their] gun and shoot him — pop him in the back of the head."

H. Pete Whidden, whose family settled in the Corkscrew Swamp in the late 1800s, hunted alligators and ran traplines throughout his life, as did his father and grandfather before him. When I talked to him in 1999, Whidden was living on the property his family had homesteaded at Corkscrew. At that time, Whidden was in his eighties. Much has changed around Corkscrew since Whidden was a young man. Today, much of the area Whidden once hunted is part of the Audubon Corkscrew Sanctuary, and the remaining land has been transformed into suburban housing developments and strip malls. So for the past several years Whidden has worked as a grocery bagger in nearby Fort Myers. On his time off, Whidden enjoyed watching the wild turkeys that congregated in his front yard and carving miniature wooden Everglades birds. When we were poking around in his barn, Whidden pulled out his gator rod. He called it his "goosin' rod," the name aptly reflecting the annoying poke intended to force agitated alligators out of their dens.

Experienced hunters could tell by the way the rod felt in their hands, by the vibration on it, whether or not they had struck an alligator after the rod passed through the ceiling of the alligator's den. In the following exchange from an interview, Whidden is trying to explain that feeling to me:

> WHIDDEN: When it [the rod] breaks in and goes into that cave, it drops. And you will learn, you can hit a cypress root or something. But if you touch that gator, you'll know it. *(Laughs.)* You get that used to it.
> OGDEN: Just the way it feels on your hand?
> WHIDDEN: Uh, hmm. Sometimes. A time or two . . . maybe where you dug the cave there'd be a root or something and it be loose and you touch it and that root would . . . *(long pause)*.
> OGDEN: Move and you'd think it was a gator?
> WHIDDEN: Yeah. And sometimes that would fool you. . . . But if that root was in the ground, pretty steady, you didn't pay much attention to it. But when you touched that gator, you knew.

Roy Overstreet echoes Whidden's sentiment, saying, "Nothing else in the world feels like a rod sliding down a gator's back."[16] The rod connected the above-ground man with the below-ground reptile, and the connection was one of movement and vibration, a charge felt through the earth. Simple objects, mundane technologies of killing, such as hooks, poles, rods, headlamps, and rifles, are constitutive of these interspecies, earthy, asymmetrical relations of becoming.

H. Pete Whidden of Corkscrew, Florida, holding a gator rod, used to locate alligators in their caves. Photograph by the author.

Stephen J. Pyne could be describing the hunter's landscape when he reminds us that "fire is extraordinarily interactive. It merges with other practices, with almost all that people do."[17] There are only a few universal human inventions, at least according to Franz Boas, and the use of fire is one of them.[18] In the Everglades, hunters were simply "crazy for setting fires," as one glades hunter told me. As they moved through and across the landscape, hunters left fire in their wake. When the mosquitoes were bad, they kept smudge pots of black mangrove slowly burning, blanketing their camps and their boats with acrid smoke that left clothes tinged with yellow. They set fires to mark their trails, to drive animals out of the saw grass, to encourage deer to fresh growth, and to make traveling easier in a "hard-walking" landscape. The hunter's landscape is one of smoldering marshland, of peat soils burning for weeks, even underground, of pinelands ablaze and crackling, and of fast-moving flames across dry prairies. The refrain of fire shaped the practice of hunting, reshaped the landscape itself, and in doing so, ordered the relationships of people and animals in the Everglades.

Pete Whidden, who told me that while hunting he constantly tossed "old red-headed" matches, explained the purposes of "making burns":

> Whenever you burn the woods, and the green grass comes up, the deer gathers there. And the deer go on that burn, licking them ashes. Before all the fire is out. I've seen that. We used to go on Little Cork-screw Island, and you could make a burn and late that evening, chances are, you'd see the deer up there. You'd see rotten logs, or something, still a smoldering, smoking. They'd come around there. They'll lick them ashes for something, pot ash, I guess.

As Whidden's description suggests, fire is a refrain of territory. Setting burns served to mark and claim territories for hunters while at the same time transforming the territories of animals. Animals, particularly deer, flocked to newly burnt lands. Glen Simmons, when talking about a friend of his in the southern Everglades during the Depression years, said, "I tell you, Ed really worked that mangrove swamp—kept it burned in patches like he was farming for deer."

Hunters understood that burning during the dry season was a dangerous practice, causing damaging fires that would burn the hammocks down to the peat. So most hunters were careful to burn only during the rainy season or to "make burns" in places where fires would not get out of control, such as along a slough or in the wet mangrove forests. Glades hunters are reverential about fire's utility, highlighting the necessity of fire to the health of the Everglades. Fire keeps the prairies and woods "cleaned out" of underbrush and encourages the renewal of plant growth. Later scientists would understand fire's crucial role in the landscape's ecological dynamics. In an early treatise on the importance of fire to the maintenance of the Everglades habitat mosaic, William B. Robertson argued that without fire, "the Everglades would no longer be the Everglades."[19] Robertson, one of Everglades National Park's pioneering biologists, was arguing against the Park Service's national management approach that encouraged the eradication of all fires within park boundaries. During summer storms, lightning strikes ignite the saw grass glades and the pinelands, producing islands of fire throughout the landscape. As Robertson's research suggested, these naturally occurring fires prevent the pinewoods and saw grass prairies from being eventually replaced by hardwood tree species. Robertson's research led to a shift in landscape management practices within the Everglades. Currently, the national park actively burns the wet prairies, pinewoods, and saw grass marshes in an effort to maintain these plant communities. This policy shift reflects an understanding of the fire-dependence of Everglades plant communities, a refrain of fire that predated the park's establishment, evoked by glades hunters as they "worked" the landscape.

For alligator hunters, fire had a special significance. For centuries, popular ideas about alligators asserted that the only thing these reptiles feared was fire.[20] In fact, if attacked by an alligator, the hapless victim's only recourse was fire, as these otherworldly creatures were believed to be immune to sword, knife, and musket shot. Fire was held to have a hypnotic quality, and when hit with the light of a flaming torch, alligators would remain passive, transfixed like a deer in a car's headlights. This belief in alligators' fear of fire may account for the initial appeal of fire-hunting, a technique that relied on the use of flaming torches to spot alligators at night. Alligators' eyes reflect a red glow when hit with a light, making alligators easily distinguishable from other nocturnal animals. Glades hunters fire-hunted on the ponds, rivers, creeks, and deeper sloughs and along the mangrove coast during the wet season, when the water was too high in the marshes to walk comfortably, as well as on moonless nights during the rest of the year. During the contemporary period, from the 1930s on, after alligator hunting became restricted in most Florida counties, nighttime hunting also afforded additional protection against game wardens. Sometimes skiffs were poled into the backcountry when waters were deeper during the rainy season and left there, hidden and kept ready for nighttime winter hunting trips. In other areas, glades hunters drove or walked across the dry marshes, then waded in waist-high water along the edge of a lake or pond, hunting on foot, a hunting strategy referred to as "shooting the lake."

The heritage of hunting with flaming torches is recalled in the continued use of the phrase "holding fire," meaning that the alligator remained captivated by a lantern's light instead of sinking below the water's surface. Regardless of the approach, by boat or on foot, hunters needed to keep noise to a minimum, as any sound would prevent the alligator from holding fire. Glen Simmons described the stealth required:

> When fire-hunting the lakes at night, you'd have to sit down in the skiff and paddle. This way you'd be on about level with them gators, and it was more steady. The [boat] pole could scare a gator if it hit a rock, and the bottom is rocky in some waters. But if you was by yourself, you'd have to lay the paddle down and pick up your gun without making any noise. When I got the skiff close enough, I'd shear off to the right of the gator just a little 'cause I shot to the left. I'd try to get within ten feet of him. 'Cause when you got your eye to the gator, sometimes you can't be sure which way he's laying when it's dark and all you can see is one eye. Though, most of the time you could tell which way he's laying. Shoot him in the eye or in the ear.[21]

Prized alligators were over ten feet long and might weigh hundreds of pounds; their skulls are long and heavy, and they have immense power in their jaws. Moreover, alligators take a while to die, as their central nervous system continues to function long after they have been shot. To prevent an alligator from sinking to the bottom of the pond as it died, hunters had to

Two men fire-hunting for alligators from a dugout canoe, 1906. The man in the bow is wearing a bull's-eye lantern, used to spot alligators at night. Photograph by Julian Dimock; printed by permission of the American Museum of Natural History.

either get the alligator into the boat or at least drag it to the bank. So while the alligator was still flailing around in the water, the hunter would grab it with a hook or by hand, hoist its head over the side of the skiff, and then use a hatchet to sever the animal's spinal cord.

The use of actual "fire" in hunting became obsolete in the late 1800s when hunters began using powerful carbide-burning lights, called bull's-eye lanterns, worn strapped to their heads. These lanterns emitted a powerful single beam that blinded or froze the alligators. Anthony W. Dimock, a wealthy sportsman and adventure writer, described fire-hunting for alligators in the

Everglades at the turn of the last century. Dimock was particularly impressed with the hypnotic power of bull's eye's beam, saying, "[It] holds helpless the reptile as the gleaming eye of the snake is reputed to fascinate (but probably doesn't) the fluttering bird."[22] The bull's-eye lantern captured dark space, transforming it into a hunter's landscape. This transformation entailed making visible the territories and territorial practices of animals, particularly alligators, while at the same time claiming those territories as their own.

FLESH (BECOMING ALLIGATOR)

Laying claim to the flesh of alligators was perhaps the most significant territorial practice in the hunter's landscape. For it was the alligator hides, or at least the cash these hides brought in, that led glades hunters to spend weeks at a time in the backcountry. Transforming live alligators into a marketable commodity was a process that began in the hot and buggy swamps of the southern Everglades and ended hundreds of miles away at commercial tanneries in Louisiana and New York. Later in this book, I examine the market and distribution networks critical to this stage in the production process. Here, prior to the antiseptics of supply and demand, let us consider the disquieting facts of the flesh. Within this refrain, hunters mimic alligators and immerse themselves in the bodies of alligators. Certainly a refrain of transformation, hunters become, or nearly so, alligators.

The refrain of flesh is, in part, acoustic. Once when I was walking with Glen Simmons along the Anhinga Trail in Everglades National Park, he began to call up the alligators, an alligator hunter's age-old trick called "grunting." The Anhinga Trail is a slightly elevated boardwalk that skirts a slough a few miles from the park's southern entrance. The Anhinga Trail is easy walking, unlike the majority of the park, and from the trail a visitor can see a striking abundance of wildlife without getting muddy or wet. For these reasons, the trail is generally crowded with amateur wildlife photographers, loaded down with gear sufficient for a National Geographic exploration, as well as young families, children running amok, and retirees out for an afternoon stroll. On that day, Simmons and I paused to peer into a still pool of water. Only a few archaic garfish hovered along the shallows, though white-plumed herons and squawking cormorants perched above in the limbs of overarching pond apples. After only a few minutes of Simmons's grunting, all at once several large alligators emerged from the depths of the still water, mesmerized and heading toward the trail's shallow banks. Simmons was ninety-one years old then. That afternoon we had only walked a few hundred yards, as Simmons had become somewhat frail in the preceding several years. Yet this ability to command action out of wild alligators, so simply and without fanfare, cheered Simmons immensely—as did the cries of alarm that quickly circulated among the bystanders.

Imitating the grunting sounds made by baby alligators was one of the surest ways of getting an adult alligator to emerge from its earthen den. Writing at the turn of the last century, the ornithologist Charles Cory described this process: "After two or three grunts . . . one or more alligators would rise to the surface and lay looking at us for a moment. The hunter has to shoot quickly under these circumstances, as the alligator soon discovers the deception and will not come up a second time for any amount of grunting."[23] Grunting begins with a nasal croaking sound formed at the back of the throat, punctuated with moments of silence, and shaped with a slightly higher pitch at the end of each call. Soft and low, alligator grunting is a gentle reverberation that forges a territorial connection between the animal and human worlds. These calls are a form of trans-species communication, practices that, as Eduardo Kohn has described, are "more than cultural, yet are not exactly noncultural."[24]

Through the acoustics of becoming alligator, hunters embodied the territorial practices of adult alligators. The ultimate goal, of course, was to claim the actual bodies of these animals, or at least the animals' skins. Skinning alligators was physically taxing and repetitious. If hunting at night, hunters would leave the skinning until first light. Waking after a few hours of sleep, hunters often skinned several dozen alligators at a time. Many of these animals weighed over a hundred pounds. Moreover, the work had to be done with speed and secrecy, as alligator hunting was largely an underground economic activity (an apt term, considering the animals' habitat). For this reason, hunters worked fast, quickly removing only the alligator's soft underbelly skin, though this varied depending upon market demand and the size and condition of the animal, a discussion I return to in a later chapter.

An unidentified man grunts for baby alligators along the Broad River, Everglades, 1906.
Photograph by Julian Dimock; printed by permission of the American Museum of Natural History.

After the skins were removed and cleaned, they could then be rolled up and stashed in some underbrush, far from the hunter's backcountry camp. Moving the hides was critical, as within hours of the skinning, scores of vultures would flock to the remaining carcasses, circling and soaring in the air above, a distinct signal for any passing game warden. Kirk Munroe, describing an alligator-hunting trip he took in 1892 with some Seminole people, recalled the post-skinning landscape: "Buzzards by the thousand assembled in the daytime, gorging themselves [on the carcasses] until they could hardly fly; while the night was made hideous by the snarlings and cries of wildcats and other beasts of prey quarrelling over the loathsome feast."[25]

Skinning alligators was a highly valued skill, and an undamaged hide was considered a mark of a competent hunter. Talk about skinning returns constantly to the theme of damage control. Since hides were priced by length, some hunters would try to excessively stretch their hides, causing the scales to begin to separate. Other sloppy tricks caused hide damage. For instance, a hunter might "shoe-string" the alligator, meaning that if the hunter was in a hurry, instead of removing the entire underbelly skin, cutting right along the tougher back scales, he would remove a narrower strip of the underbelly skin, hoping no one would be the wiser. For the most part, hide damage was beyond the skinner's control, consisting of such blemishes as preexisting marks on the hide or the presence of bony plates in the hide, called "buttons," common to Florida alligators.

Because alligator muscles continue to contract for days after death, without intervention the animal's twitching could result in a hunter's damaging the hide while removing it. To prevent this from happening, the first steps in the process required severing these neuromuscular connections. Hunters did this by first cutting into the animal's back, near the hindquarters, then shoving their knives into the alligator's backbone. Although the animal was dead, its remaining reflexes would cause it to rear up and break its own backbone. Hunters then would collect plants from the surrounding gator holes, such as thick-stalked ferns they called "gator-rod ferns," and after stripping the plants' leaves, they would run the stalks up and down the animal's spine, beginning at the hind end and working upward toward the skull. As Simmons explained, "If you didn't take the wiggle out of him with the fern, his muscles would twitch for half the day, and his hide would draw up to where you could damage the hide when you was skinning him."

Hide buyers carefully inspected each hide before setting their price, reducing the price on hides considered "damaged" by nicks or knife marks, overstretching, shoe-stringing, or discolorations caused in the drying process. For these reasons, hunters considered damaged hides as animals and time partially wasted. In many ways, a hunter's reputation (and identity) corresponded to his ability to skin an alligator quickly and without nicking or damaging the hide. Though there were exceptions, most backcountry people looked down on outsiders who hunted for sport or other forms of what they considered "wanton killing." The backcountry's ethical code required that all animals that were taken be used for food or cash. In the hunter's landscape, what it means to be a *man* is constituted through a relationship with animals and through an ethics of animal flesh.

Pete Whidden told me a story about his father that illustrates this point. When Whidden was four or five years old, his father was out with a few men driving around in the woods in a Model T "skeeter," a cut-down car with no doors or top. As the men rounded a corner, they hit a stump in the road, and Whidden's father was thrown from the car. The accident left Whidden's father with a silver plate in his head and paralyzed on the right side of his body. For the rest of his life, Whidden's father used a crutch, dragged his right leg, and kept his right arm tucked in his shirt. Whidden ended his story saying, "He go and camp in the woods by himself and he could skin a gator, or otter, 'coon." Whidden is a man of few words, and he told me this story to convey what he considered an essential truth about his father. His father was a man who, against all odds — crippled, living in a remote settlement in the Corkscrew Swamp during the lean years between World Wars I and II — could still provide for his family. He did this by skinning animals.

Flesh, as it emerges in the refrain of skinning, is intimate with sensate properties other than acoustic. Tactile and odorous, it is a refrain of hands grappling in blood and shit. Simmons continued, describing to me the final stages of skinning:

> Sometimes there would be a little blood on them, but that didn't hurt anything. But sometimes they were too nasty 'cause they had messed on themselves when you skinned them. You keep your foot on his belly when you're skinning him, and you're squeezing stuff out of him. Then we'd try to wash him — 'cause it smells so bad.[26]

The hunter's landscape is one of bare hands and bare feet immersed in the flesh of alligators.

The refrain of flesh is that of becoming alligator — of sounding like alligator, smelling like alligator, and covering oneself in alligator. This becoming, while at the same time remaining the same, endows the refrain of flesh with mimetic qualities. Michael Taussig has described mimesis as "the nature that culture uses to create second nature, the faculty to copy, imitate, make models, explore difference, yield into and become Other."[27] For Taussig, mimesis is not just copying or becoming Other; it is the enactment of that strange tactile space between two poles of difference. In other words, mimesis embodies difference and sameness simultaneously.

In many ways all the territorial refrains within the hunter's landscape enact the curious schizophrenia of mimesis—what Deleuze and Guattari have described as becoming animal. To become animal is "never a reproduction or an imitation."[28] Instead, becoming animal entails a transformative crossing of thresholds of intensities. These movements establish new articulations of the human and nonhuman worlds. In the hunter's landscape, the territorial practices of humans and nonhumans entangle and reshape each other, producing a new landscape that is both sameness and difference.

CONCLUSION: NARROW ESCAPES

The hunter's landscape is an assemblage where refrains forge territorial connections among people, objects, and animals. The refrains I have explored here are elemental and basic: earth, fire, and flesh. Indeed, from an ecological and biological perspective, these refrains are central features of the Everglades and of life itself. Quite literally, the practice of hunting engages the material conditions of world making.

Yet at the same time, these refrains reverberate far beyond the geospatial boundaries of the Everglades and the culture of hunting, a critical point about how refrains work. Refrains do not only define and create assemblages of the human and nonhuman worlds; they also transform places, experiences, and ideas situated outside territory. Deleuze and Guattari describe certain refrains as conductors that order the passage from one milieu to another.[29] They shift the register, so to speak, among heterogeneous spacetimes. Although this chapter has been grounded in space and time, rhizomes, we should always remember, are less fixed. As this book seeks to map these movements within the Everglades as rhizome, I end this chapter with a movement of deterritorialization, a locus where a refrain orders the passage of the hunter's landscape to places and peoples outside the landscape's immediate geography.

In the hunter's landscape, the refrains of earth and flesh often conspire to become another refrain, one we might call the refrain of "narrow escape."

Even after rifles became common in alligator hunting, glades hunters spent a considerable amount of time attempting to drag alligators from their dens by hand, even crawling into dens after the alligator when necessary. Consider this story Pete Whidden told me about capturing a live eleven-foot alligator, which he later sold to the Everglades Wonder Gardens, a tourist attraction in Bonita Springs, Florida. Whidden and his Uncle Stanley often hunted alligators together. Generally they would hunt for a week or so for hides and then capture forty to fifty smaller alligators and sell them to the Piper brothers, who owned the Everglades Wonder Gardens. At that time, Whidden was driving a cut-down Model A Ford truck that had a pen in the truck's bed for hauling live alligators out of the swamp.

In this story, Whidden and his Uncle Stanley trailed an alligator for two days. It was a dry time of the year, so the alligator had taken refuge within a den located in a hammock in the Fakahatchee Strand, a twenty-mile-long slough in the Big Cypress Swamp. The men could tell the den's layout included a five-foot tunnel that turned and opened up into a cave. As the ground was rocky, the men planned to break through the den's rock ceiling from above using a sledgehammer. But before expending that much effort, they had to make sure the alligator was actually in the den. So Whidden, a few years younger than his uncle, crawled into the mouth of the den and, on his stomach, inched his way back along the den's narrow passage. As Whidden rounded the curve in the den's tunnel, he came face to face with the alligator. When telling this story, Whidden held his hand several inches from his face and said, "His nose was about that far from mine, when I peeked around the corner." The men had prearranged that if Whidden started kicking his feet, Stanley was to rapidly pull him out. When Whidden came in contact with the alligator, he immediately started backing out of the den. Seeing Whidden moving quickly, Stanley yanked him out of the cave, dragging him across the rocks and leaving him bloody and bruised. Eventually the men captured the alligator. They did so by breaking up the straight section of the den with the sledgehammer, then lassoing the alligator around the neck, and tying it to an oak tree.

The hunter's landscape is charged with the refrain of the narrow escape. I have heard stories of large alligators trailing hunters back to their camps, after dark, when the men were asleep, as well as countless tales of alligators upsetting boats, leaving men to swim to shore in alligator-filled waters. Yet the narrow escape, a refrain constituted by earth and flesh, also forms a recurring narrative trope in Florida's larger adventure and exploration literature. For instance, in 1794, William Bartram described a close encounter with a decidedly fantastic alligator that roared and belched "water and smoke" as it attacked his boat.[30] Over a century later, Van Campen Heilner, an associate editor for *Field and Stream* magazine, provided a vivid, and fairly hyperbolic, description of a narrow escape in an account entitled "Death Struggle with an Alligator."[31]

While searching for a bird rookery near Madeira Hammock, now within Everglades National Park, Heilner and his guide Henry waded through an alligator hole intent upon taking close-up photographs of the resident alligator. In his account, as Heilner attempted to escape the attacking alligator, he slipped in the mud, providing an opportunity for the alligator to grab Heilner by the leg and drag him under the water. Heilner only escaped after frantically stabbing the alligator in the eye. The alligator then released Heilner's leg, and in a matter of seconds, bleeding and feeble, Heilner was able to grab his rifle and shoot the alligator before the author sunk exhaustedly "down into the awful slime."[32] Whether told by hunters or by adventurers, the narrow escape is always the same.

Glades hunters are well aware of alligator hunting's archetypal resonance and power. Their narrow escape stories transform the hunter's landscape into an enfabled landscape charged with mythic potential. These stories serve as vectors of escape from the territorial boundaries of the Everglades and the messy, physically exhausting, and often mundane tasks of killing. They link the hunter's landscape to the larger canon of the man–beast encounter and transform the Everglades in the process. When told by rural hunters, these narrow-escape stories offered a moment of social cachet, granted by a larger society that undervalued the lives of backcountry, often undereducated, people. In forging this vector of escape, the refrain of narrow escape enacts a movement of deterritorialization, a leaving of the constraints of territoriality, like crayfish that, as Deleuze and Guattari describe them, "set off walking in file at the bottom of the ocean."[33]

The Theatrics of Everglades Outlaws

> This attempt to do a low-budget, regional variation on *Bonnie and Clyde* is likeably earnest but has little else to offer.
>
> —CRAIG BUTLER, review of *Little Laura and Big John* (1973), *All Movie Guide*

After DeSoto Tiger's body was discovered, Sheriff George Baker of Palm Beach County dispatched two deputies to bring John Ashley in for questioning. Rumors suggested Ashley was hiding out at a camp near Hobe Sound. As the deputies made their way through a heavy growth of palmettos along the Dixie Highway, John Ashley and his brother Bob suddenly appeared and held the lawmen at gunpoint. After disarming the deputies, John Ashley sent a message to their boss, saying, "Tell Baker not to send any more chicken-hearted men with rifles or they are apt to get hurt."[1]

To avoid further confrontations, Ashley spent the next several years living out of state, first in New Orleans, then in Seattle, where he worked at a logging camp. Apparently missing his home and family, he returned to southern Florida in 1914 and peacefully surrendered to the police. Secure in the racial politics of the era, Ashley felt confident that a jury of his "peers" would acquit him of the murder. At his trial, Ashley claimed self-defense, testifying that DeSoto Tiger had threatened to shoot him if he did not give him some liquor. Ashley's strategy worked, and the judge declared a mistrial.

Hoping to seat a less sympathetic jury, the prosecutors then moved the trial to Dade County. Less sure of the outcome of a second trial, Ashley decided not to risk conviction and took flight. At the time, Bob Baker, Sheriff Baker's son, was Dade County's jailer. Ashley made his escape on a rainy evening as the pair were returning from Ashley's first day at court. In the dooryard of the jail, as Baker held a plate of food, provided by the Ashley family, and fumbled with a light and the key, Ashley took off, easily scaling the ten-foot-high chicken-wire fence that enclosed the compound. Though the jailor immediately pursued the fleeing Ashley on a bicycle, Ashley quickly vanished into the Everglades. It is within this landscape that the Ashley Gang takes form. In the Everglades, Ashley was joined by Clarence Middleton, an opium addict; Kid Low, a bank robber; members of his extended family; and sundry other criminals.

An outmoded theatricality pervades the Ashley Gang story, like a Keystone Kops comedy infected with melancholia. Bicycle pursuits and jeering taunts, set within a forbidding landscape—these theatrics mark the gang's thirteen-year history. For instance, in 1915, John, Bob Ashley, and Kid Low successfully robbed the Bank of Stuart. During the confusion, Kid Low shot John Ashley in the face. The bullet shattered Ashley's jaw and lodged near his eye. Though the gang escaped into the Everglades, Sheriff Baker was tipped to Ashley's location after hearing that a doctor had been called to treat Ashley's wounds. Two of DeSoto Tiger's brothers (Naha and Tom Tiger) helped lead the posse to Ashley's hidden camp.[2] There they found John Ashley being tended by his brother Bill. In great pain, John was taken to the Palm Beach jail, where a doctor removed Ashley's damaged eye and fit him with a glass one.

This glass eye became a tragic touchstone in the Ashley drama. Bob Baker, the hapless jailor, succeeded his father as sheriff of Palm Beach County. In the following years, Sheriff Baker endured humiliation by the Ashley Gang. Under his watch, gang members repeatedly escaped from jail and prison, robbed banks, sold illegal liquor, and hijacked the supplies of other rumrunners. Throughout, Ashley taunted Sheriff Baker. In return, Sheriff Baker vowed to wear Ashley's glass eye as a watch fob. After Ashley was killed, a deputy sheriff at the scene knelt over Ashley's body and removed the slain man's eye and brought it, like proof of a vanquished Cyclops, back to Sheriff Baker. Years later, that deputy told Ada Williams, "But do you know... they made us send it back so that it could be buried with his body? If I'd known that, I'd have smashed it under my heel on the bridge that night."[3] Indeed, Ashley's grief-stricken family did demand the eye's return for burial.

Although I have foreshadowed the story's bitter conclusion, many of the gang's misadventures and narrow escapes provide comic relief. For example, during one of John Ashley's stints at the Florida State Prison at Raiford, his young nephew, Hanford Mobley, led a second robbery of the Stuart bank. This time, Mobley, described as "frail and effeminate," gained entrance to the bank by disguising himself as a woman (a theatrical trope signaling levity). Mobley wore a white blouse, a long black skirt, a hat, and a veil draped over his face—this to hide the "determined leer of a killer."[4] Still, the sight of a veil-wearing woman, no doubt an anomaly in this rural Florida town, should have raised some alarm at the bank. Later that day, the police found Hanford's costume in an abandoned car about twenty-two miles north of Stuart.

The film *Little Laura and Big John* (1973) focused on the "doomed lovers" aspect of the Ashley Gang saga, though the film also captures the story's camp, albeit inadvertently. In the film, Karen Black of *Easy Rider* fame played the role of Laura Upthegrove. As is the practice of Hollywood cinema, the real Upthegrove was much heartier than the winsome actress. Hix C. Stuart, whose version of the Ashley story remains the most comprehensive, described Upthegrove's appearance as Amazonian, weather-beaten, and unkempt.[5] She was also a force to be reckoned with, wearing a .38 caliber revolver strapped to her waist, her "every command obeyed."[6]

In all probability, Upthegrove first met John Ashley through her stepbrother, Joe Tracey, who was also a gang member. So many of this story's characters are enmeshed in a confusing network of relations, a rhizome. For instance, Tracey met John Ashley during an early stint in Raiford Prison. Tracey was later returned to Raiford and while there married Laura Upthegrove's sister, Lola. Tracey died at Raiford on the eve of his release. The midwife who brought Tracey into this world, and who sheltered him from the law, was also the mother-in-law of one of the deputies involved in the case. Upthegrove's own family was equally messy. Upthegrove was estranged from her husband, E. A. Tillman, when she met John Ashley. Her two children remained with their father after the marriage fell apart. Upthegrove must have been bothered to some extent by this alienation from her children because in 1923 she, John Ashley, and Ashley's teenage nephew attempted to kidnap the children from their father's home. According to Stuart, the trio drove over to Tillman's Indiantown home and, seeing that Tillman was gone, bundled the children into the car and took off. Eventually, Tillman tracked the group to the home of Upthegrove's father. There, although everyone was loaded

Burl Ives, holding moonshine and a snake, plays a threatening Everglades outlaw and poacher named Cottonmouth in Nicholas Ray's film *Wind across the Everglades* (1958).

down with weaponry, Ashley and Tillman resorted to brawling.[7] I imagine the children watching this scene, frightened as their parents screamed insults, the men grappling bloody on the floor. When the fight ended, Tillman left and took the children with him. In the vast Ashley Gang oeuvre, this is the only mention of Upthegrove's children.

Over time, the Ashley Gang story, as with many historical narratives, has become condensed to a recitation of dramatic scenes—producing a cinematic sense of the past. The film *Little Laura and Big John* reproduced the theatrics of the dominant Ashley Gang historiography, a gun-toting couple-gone-bad love story set in the Florida swamps. Yet these theatrics do little but offer us a selective vision of the rural poor. A critical moment in Nicholas

Ray's film *Wind across the Everglades* (1958) is more overt in its dichotomizing displacements of rural white culture from the Everglades. In this scene, Walt Murdock, a young and impassioned game warden played by Christopher Plummer, leans against the mast of a sloop docked at a trading post in the Everglades backcountry. He explains to the family who runs the trading post, which includes his future love interest, and to a pro-development dandy from Miami why he must single-handedly rescue the Everglades from a dangerous band of poachers bent on annihilating the region's plume birds:

> It [the Everglades] is sort of the way the world must have looked on the first day, when it was all water, and then the first land beginning to rise out of the sea, you feel the life force in there, in its purest, earliest form. Then Cain and the brothers of Cain raised their twelve-gauge shotguns and fired into the face of God.

Though Ray's film debuted a half century after plume-bird hunting ended in the Everglades, clearly its wilderness vision, with its attendant holy-war narrative, continued to resonate within the popular imagination. This is the selective vision of pure nature. This is the selective vision of empire.

4. THE TRAVELS OF SNAKES, MANGROVES, AND MEN

Statues beckon you from gardens and public parks; you walk onwards
with fleeting glances for everything, for everything in motion and
at rest, for hackney cabs, which rumble along indolently, for the
electric tram, which is now beginning to run and from out of which
people's eyes look down at you, for the idiotic helmet of a constable,
for a person with ragged shoes and trousers, for a man undoubtedly
of once comfortable circumstances who sweeps the street in a fur
coat and top hat, for all things, just as you yourself are for all things
a fleeting sight.

—ROBERT WALSER, "Good Day, Giantess"

There is no stillness in Robert Walser's landscapes. Instead, his prose
meanders along country lanes and through forest meadows, with hardly a
pause for the bustle of a village's town square. Walser was born in Biel, Swit-
zerland, in 1878, and when not writing in sparsely furnished rented rooms,
he spent much of his life out walking. His prose reflects a life, Susan Sontag
has suggested, spent "obsessively turning time into space."[1] Though Walser
enjoyed some literary success during his lifetime, with both Franz Kafka and
Robert Musil among his admirers, he abandoned writing in 1933 after his
forced relocation from the Waldau Mental Asylum, where he had committed himself in 1929, to another institution in the Swiss canton of Appenzell.[2]
Walser had been diagnosed with schizophrenia, though his biographers suggest that little evidence supports this diagnosis. Instead, Walser seems to have
been a deeply solitary man who became increasingly overwhelmed with the
complexities of the world around him. He spent the last decades of his life

An egret taking flight.
Photograph by Deborah Mitchell.

institutionalized, dying during one of his long walks on a snowy Christmas Day in 1956. Walking apparently brought Walser both contentment and solace, perhaps accounting for his unrivaled ability to portray the mobility of landscape experience.

Even when Walser's characters are at rest, such as gazing out a bedroom window, the world around is cinematic in its motion. Much of Walser's short prose pieces are meditations on the mundane activities that define daily life — fastening a button, drinking a cup of coffee, taking an afternoon walk through a park. Read as a whole, Walser's work offers a phenomenology of domesticity and domesticated nature, capturing the gestures and movements that define our encounters with the world. Walter Benjamin described Walser's prose as "running wild," referring to Walser's mostly unedited method, a stream-of-consciousness technique that apparently privileged the process of writing over standard literary conventions.[3] At times, Walser's prose does feel like wildness barely constrained, where "lines of flight," to use Deleuze and Guattari's phrase, are pursued along unanticipated changes of course.[4] Although Walser was misdiagnosed as schizophrenic, his prose exhibits a kind of schizoid logic appropriate to the mapping of movement through a rhizomic landscape. His insights inform this chapter in several ways.

First, landscapes are experienced by *bodies in motion*. Barbara Bender has proposed that landscapes represent "time materializing," noting, "Landscapes, like time, never stand still."[5] At first glance, glades hunters' memories of the landscape seem frozen in time — a time before the establishment of the national park, before the transformation of much of the Everglades into housing developments and strip malls, or before alligator hunting became an untenable livelihood. These sepia-tinged events certainly transformed the material culture and subsistence strategies of locals living in the Everglades, consequently shaping their sense of place. Yet as a corollary to Bender's assertion, the hunter's landscape materializes because they, *the hunters*, rather than just time, *kept moving*. Mobility critically shaped glades hunters' production of place.

Second, we neither move through abstract space nor practice abstract forms of movement. Tim Cresswell distinguishes "movement" from "mobility," defining the latter as the "dynamic equivalent of *place*."[6] For Cresswell, mobility is movement that is socially produced, saturated with cultural meaning and the power dynamics of cultural difference. Far more complex than the complicated synaptic firing that directs bodies in motion, mobility is movement specific to a particular time and place. For instance, Walser's investigations of town and country build upon the tradition of the flaneur, the "ur-form of the modern intellectual," as Susan Buck-Morss has described the figure.[7] In early-twentieth-century intellectual culture, epitomized most notably in Walter Benjamin's famous Arcades Project, the flaneur acted as a sympathetic observer of modern life, studying the people and places of the city while strolling the city streets. Some of the Walser's best "walserings," or short experimental prose pieces, mirror a tour guide's steady patter: here we come to the train station, now we encounter a woman waiting for her lover on a park bench, here is the local pub, and so on. No doubt Walser walked for multiple reasons — health, compulsion, romantic visions of man and nature — yet both Walser's mobility and his representations of that mobility must be understood as in dialogue with a specific cultural and literary tradition.

As I explore in chapter 6, the political economy of the hide and pelt market certainly guided glades hunters' landscape practices. Hunters chose their routes and destinations within the Everglades based on game availability, or perceived availability, and changing market demands (for raccoon hides and flat-skinned alligators, for example). Yet at the same time, hunters were moving through a landscape that was meaningful beyond this economic imperative. Rather than being an abstract space, the Everglades was lively with cultural, political, and personal histories. Walser's poetics reminds us that this multiplicity is inescapably entangled in the landscape. As Walser's characters move through the landscape, images both real and imaginary become manifest; with each step we take along a country road, memories of the past transform the present; giants and trolls beckon the "unreliable" narrator even while the present recedes methodically behind. The Everglades is alive with histories of people dead and living, with morality tales of local justice and girls gone bad, and with uncanny phenomena, such as the unnaturally large snakes I write about in this chapter. All these detours, and many more, shaped the mobility, or immobility, of local landscape practices.

Last, it is not only humans that are mobile. Alligators, nutrients, charged particles, vegetal matter, and the like, humans' fellow travelers, are also on the move. Expanding upon Walter Benjamin's work, Michael Taussig has argued that between "construction" and "essentialism" lies another episte-mological zone.[8] We might understand this space of knowing as a sort of "contact zone," where bodies, geographies, biota, and mythologies engage in overlapping mobilities. The contact zone is charged with tactile encounters: the distant sight of circling vultures, the acrid smell of alligator scat, the bite of a saw grass thicket — neither prefiguring culture (essential) nor culturally determined (constructed). Instead, the contact zone is marked by a furious exchange of messages, territorializing acts, and countermoves, all taking place among and between the human and nonhuman worlds. Something gets lost in all our hand-wringing over culture's abstraction from nature or the trou-bling Great Divide between nature and culture that marks modernity, even with the understanding that the boundaries of these divisions are always under siege by various hybrid forms.[9] Although I do not disagree with the claim that these divisionary tactics are *fundamental* to our understanding of the West's intellectual history and related colonialist practices,[10] I would like to move on and explore the mysterious politics of the nonhuman. Nature produces its own lines of flight. Or as Walser put it, "Nature demands its rights everywhere."[11] This chapter offers a graphic tour of bodies moving through a space where nature is staking her own claims and producing her own countermoves.

WALKING AND WAITING

Traveling the Everglades was always slow going, with seasonal changes to the landscape shaping the work of turning time into space. During the dry winter season, the open glades form basins of shallow water; in some places and years the water dries up completely, leaving a white crust of dried algae mats across the sun-baked earth, mats that locals humorously refer to as "snow." When the Everglades was dry, or relatively so, hunters spent long days walking this parched earth to reach areas of deeper water where wild-life congregated, such as in lakes, ponds, and alligator holes. Walkers could not haul enough supplies on their backs for a several-week trip, particu-larly the amount of salt required to prepare alligator hides. So when "walk-hunting," as it was called, hunters set up camps not too far from one of the roads that traversed the Everglades interior or near a deep canal. From these base camps, hunters walked the swamp all day, returning at nightfall to eat, prepare their hides, and sleep until daybreak.

Though the popular image of the Everglades may be that of a vast grassy swamp, the walker's terrain varied substantially. In some places, getting into the backcountry involved negotiating miles of "pinnacle rock," a Swiss-cheese expanse of rough limestone crags that form foot-sized islands within the marl prairies. Deeper basins, called "solution holes," are interspersed throughout the pinnacle rock, their size ranging from a few inches deep to twenty feet deep and wide. Travel in the rocky glades requires a constant adjustment of stride, a stuttered syncopation as the walker steps and leaps from one rough plateau to another. Thickets of vegetation, such as saw grass and scrub, often conceal solution holes below, so in seeking solid ground the walker takes tentative steps along a meandering course of rock and crevasse.

Marjory Stoneman Douglas, the landscape's most famous advocate, described the prairies of the Everglades in these terms:

> The miracle of the light pours over the green and brown expanse of saw grass and of water, shining and slow-moving below, the grass and water that is the meaning and central fact of the Everglades of Florida. It is a river of grass.[12]

Saw grass, *Cladium jamaicense,* and water remain the central fact of the Everglades, though from the walker's perspective the meaning of this central fact was surely less idyllic than Douglas's description suggests. Saw grass, which is technically a sedge, grows to heights of nine feet, particularly in the muck soils found in the northern Everglades. It is the dominant plant species in the Everglades, and in certain areas it presents itself as a thick wall of vegetation. These saw grass marshes continually frustrated the efforts of early Everglades explorers and surveyors, who described them as "desolate" and "impenetrable." Hugh deLaussett Willoughby, writing in 1898 of his own attempts at crossing the saw grass, said, "It pays better to go twenty-five miles around than half mile through."[13]

Although saw grass's dense growth limits the movement of many species of animals, including people, alligators use these marshes for nesting during June and July, particularly in the central and southern Everglades. To reach these alligators, glades hunters would walk-hunt the saw grass country.

This entailed a constant grappling with the plant, as walkers slogged and stumbled through water that could be anywhere from a few inches to several feet deep. Sharp upwardly tilted teeth line the edge of the plant's stiff blade. When rubbed against, the blades leave painful cuts that are notoriously slow to heal. Though most people wore clothes that covered their arms and legs, exposed skin on palms, fingers, necks, faces, and, often, bare feet was unavoidably shredded by thousands of little cuts from saw grass.

Walk-hunters tended to be fairly wet much of the time. As the alligator nesting season corresponds with the rainy season in southern Florida, walk-hunters often encountered sudden afternoon showers. These rains were welcome respites from the summer heat and humidity, but they left clothes sodden and bedding damp. These storms also meant periods of delay, as glades hunters sought shelter within hammocks to wait for lightning and hard rains to pass.

Gladeland mobility involved multiple pauses along the way—side trips, obstacles, switchbacks, and *waiting*. Like a dirge, waiting's refrain appears throughout the walk-hunters' narratives. Pete Whidden described to me waiting for an alligator to rise up out of its watery cave:

> I have set for 'em as much as eight hours. And he was there, 'cause he come up. They say they can't stay down but two or three or four hours, but I know they can stay down, some of them, eight hours. . . . They can hold their air that long. Sure can. And three or four or five hours is very common. I've set for them.

Throughout those long hours, hunters remained as still as possible. Any movement or unusual sound would keep the alligator from rising from its cave. The need for caution transformed common movements to silent gestures—brushing off a horsefly, stretching cramped legs, lighting a cigarette. Hunters waited for alligators in the rain and when the sun was high overhead. Even after nightfall, waiting continued. In the evening, hunters would build a fire near the alligator's cave, hoping it would then emerge.

Something or someone must be *waited for*; thus the feeling of anticipation saturates the wait, the anticipation of seeing an alligator rise to the water's surface. Although anticipation stilled the bodies of hunters, they were at the same time fully engaged in the poetics of nature's gestures. While kneeling alongside an alligator hole, hunters became particularly attuned to the movement of water. An ever-so-slight ripple or little bubbles breaking the surface spoke to the animal's movement. When frustrated by the wait, tired hunters were apt to take chances. For instance, hunters might shoot as soon as the tip of the alligator's nose broke the water's surface. Jumping the gun in this way was risky. If the animal was only spooked, it would then rapidly return to its cave, and the waiting would begin anew.

So much about walk-hunting the Everglades landscape seems time-consuming: negotiating pinnacle rock, wading through saw grass, waiting for rains to stop and game to rise. In *The Production of Space*, Henri Lefebvre laments the invisibility of time in modern society.[14] Time, according to Lefebvre, leaves no traces and is experienced only as movement. Yet in the hunter's landscape, time, like mobility, is not continuous — it is not like the calibrated movement of the hands on a clock. Nature imposes a reptilian crawl on the passage of time, so much waiting alligators out.

SNAKES AND HUMANS

Nonhuman forms of life, both real and imaginary, also move *to and fro* within the Everglades landscape, intersecting and interfering with the mobilities of glades hunters. Plants, birds, algae, fish, snails, and certainly alligators move about and reshape the hunter's landscape in the process. These diverse practices of mobility assert an agency over the assemblage. In other words, these practices are a politics of nature that have the capacity to entangle the world-making relations of humans and nonhumans. Within the hunter's landscape, snakes have a particular power.

The Everglades teems with at least twenty-five different snake species. Mangrove prop roots conceal coiled cottonmouths; water snakes of many colors and dispositions zip through marshes and canals; diamondback rattlers and coral snakes take shelter within the hammocks and pinewoods. The appearance of a snake often interrupted the movement of people in the Everglades, and the possibility of snakes certainly shaped the way people moved. Glades hunters' gestural repertoire included "watching your step," shaking out blankets, and prodding the forest litter with a stick. Skiffers were adept at using their poles to pluck from the boat the many snakes that dropped in from overarching limbs. Some hunters sold live snakes, particularly venomous ones, to zoos and roadside attractions. To catch a moccasin or rattlesnake, I am told, you first grab the snake by its tail, quickly whip the snake around, then pin it between your legs. Next, you pull the snake through your legs until you may safely grab its head. Even with these techniques and with many precautions, for Everglades hunters being struck at and bitten by snakes was a common occurrence. Everyone has a story of dealing with snake bites, from backcountry first aid to rushed trips to the hospital.

Marilyn Nissenson and Susan Jonas, in their book of snake mythology, conjure the snake in terms that evoke the multiplicity of a rhizome:

> Snakes slither. They are silent. They come and go without warning. They look slimy. Snakes have no differentiated body parts — no neck or limbs. Their eyes never close, and their expressions do not change. They are cold-blooded. They have a forked tongue. Baby snakes have no charm; they look like their parents, only smaller. Snakes are hard to anthropomorphize. They are mysterious, remote — the Other.
>
> Snakes crawl on the earth — a permanently debased condition. They are associated with the dank, moldy floor of the forest. They lurk in tall grass and strike without warning; they drop from trees and squeeze their victims to death before swallowing them whole.[15]

When describing the symbolic importance of snakes to the snake-handling religious practices of southern Christian sects, Weston La Barre maps the movement of snakes: they disrupt dreams, poison the milk of nursing mothers, and emerge from the mouths of those suffering from hexes. A snake's untimely death may cause torrential rains and overflowing stream banks. Snakes are lightning and fire. Snakes can charm, "fascinate," and emanate offensive and sickening odors.[16] If mobility is essentially a process of *displacement,* then snakes have the power of *dislocation,* or, put another way, snakes transfer and transfigure humans into realms of the uncanny. As E. O. Wilson describes this potent magic, a snake "appears without warning and departs abruptly, leaving behind not a specific memory of any real snake but the vague sense of a more powerful creature."[17]

Although the movements of humans and snakes intersect in multiple locations and in multiple ways in the Everglades, encounters with "unnaturally large" snakes form their own entanglements. Such phenomenal creatures figure throughout Everglades local history, their narrative primacy perhaps only challenged by tales of alligator savagery. For instance, in 1897 the *Miami Metropolis* reported that Walter Ralston, a "snake-charmer of wide reputation," captured a twelve-foot boa constrictor at Black Point, along the mangrove coast. The article's author hoped that the boa's capture would put an end to the "untold fabrications and exaggerations of snake stories" told for the past fifteen years in the area.[18] But the snake's capture did little to lessen the snake mania. Only two days later, a front-page article in the *New York Times* described Ralston's "death struggle" with the serpent, though now the snake had become transformed into a thirty-three-foot-long python.[19]

Encounters with snakes considered unnaturally large very nearly derailed early exploration in the Everglades. The account of one of the first great Everglades expeditions, led by Major Archie Williams in 1883, contains one such encounter. Wolf Hollander, the expedition's artist, reported being chased by a snake described as being of "enormous size and quite ferocious." When Major Williams asked Hollander why he had not shot the creature, the New Orleans artist said, "De rifle maybe snap, and de snake bit me, *but de legs I know he don't snap.*"[20]

A year later, James Henshall, a physician and naturalist from Kentucky, testified to another sighting of an outsized snake. Taking a break from his naturalist explorations, Henshall stopped at Panther Key, within the Ten Thousand Islands off the southwestern coast of the Everglades, where he visited with John Gomez and his wife. "Old Man Gomez" as he was called, was an unnaturally large figure in his own right, who reportedly served with Napoleon Bonaparte, acted as a cabin boy for the pirate Gasparilla, and fought in the Seminole War.[21] While they were talking, Gomez's wife told Henshall of a horrifying encounter with a fifteen-foot-long rattlesnake:

> Oh dear! . . . I can see it now! Oh-h-h! Such a snake! Such a snake! 'Twas as long as this room; it was; it was; it was! I can see it now! I can see it now! . . . Oh, it makes me sick! It makes me sick! I can smell it too! I can smell it too! It was as big as a water bucket! It was, it was, it was! Oh-h-h! Such a snake! Such a snake! Such a snake![22]

One would imagine that Mrs. Gomez was a hardy woman, used to the rigors of backcountry living. After all, the couple had named their island Panther Key after the cats that had finally put an end to their attempts at goat farming. Yet the presence of this large snake, unseen and yet so vivid, haunted Mrs. Gomez's memories and the landscape itself.

Several years later, this snake, or another just like it, made an appearance on an island miles from Panther Key. In a report published in a Miami newspaper in 1896, Ed Brewer, a glades hunter, witnessed what he described as a huge serpent. Brewer was guiding a hunting party of well-off city folk, including a judge. In the newspaper account, the snake lay in the water, its eyes projecting a beam of bright and unworldly light, all the while "smacking his huge chops."[23] Paralyzed by a combination of fear, the snake's mesmerizing power, and whiskey's magical realism, the party was unable to shoot the creature. The following year, Brewer overcame his inhibitions, reportedly killing a very large snake in the same area. Unfortunately, Brewer was unable to retrieve the snake's skin, as the "sickening" odor emanating from its dead body rendered Brewer unconscious.

Lieutenant Hugh Willoughby decided to investigate Brewer's story as well as the reliability of the many sensational stories circulating in the winter of 1897 about the "Land of the Big Snake." So before embarking on their own expedition across the Everglades, Willoughby and Brewer took a side trip to recover the remains of Brewer's kill. According to Willoughby, the site resembled the Amazon River—tropically lush, with an "earthy, snaily smell," one of the "snakiest" places Willoughby had ever seen.[24] There, they discovered the partial skeletal remains of what looked to be a very large snake, dispersed across a wide area, though the skull was missing. A snake professional at the University of Pennsylvania later confirmed that Willoughby's specimen was a big snake, probably an eight-foot-long rattler.

Uncle Steve Roberts, of the Everglades fishing village of Flamingo, told reporters from the Florida Writers' Project that this serpent "wasn't no legend but a fact."[25] In Roberts's story, a Seminole named Buster Farrel had killed the snake in 1892. Farrel's first indication of unworldly presence was the sight of a beaten path through the grass. Thinking it was a "whopping big 'gator,'" Farrel followed the drag line and encountered a large snake. Though the snake lay more than a rifle shot from Farrel, he fired anyway. The snake thrashed off, making more noise "than a hurricane." Several days later, circling buzzards led Farrel to the scattered remains of the dead serpent. Even with the carcass in tatters, Farrel swore that the snake was "60 feet long and as big as a barrel."

In the hunter's landscape, snakes, real and mythic, staked their claims on the landscape. In doing so, these snakes altered the mobility of local hunters, settlers, visiting explorers, and naturalists. These snakes had the power to mesmerize, to halt people in their tracks; they create their own lines of flight, disrupting and redirecting the spatial practices of people in the Everglades.

SPATIAL DISCOURSES: MOVING "TO AND FRO"

Although all forms of hunting required a great deal of walking, glades hunters preferred to travel by boat. When the water is high, the Everglades interior feels less like a river of grass than like a grassy freshwater sea. Hunters glided across these grassy seas or used their boats to work their way through sloughs, creeks, and rivers to reach the lakes and ponds of the drier interior. At all times of year, the coastal mangroves are inaccessible without a boat, and so the only way to reach places like the Bill Ashley Jungles was by boat.

Hunters traveled through and across the Everglades using an established network of intersecting passageways. Although these passageways certainly facilitated movement, I am particularly interested in how traveling along these passages became another way of knowing the landscape. We might understand this spatial practice as one that produced a residential *discourse of the landscape*. Roland Barthes reminds us that the etymology of the word "discourse" comes from the Latin *discurrere,* meaning to "run to and fro."[26] Hunters moved to and fro along these skiff passages, and as they traveled, they experienced an Everglades rich with cultural memory. Nature also moves to and fro and thus engages in her own spatial practices. We generally consider discourse as a kind of language that encompasses words, actions, and various materialities. Everglades mobility is a spatial discourse that reveals the entanglements of people, memory, and nature on the move.

Glade boats, called skiffs, were generally homemade, cobbled together from discarded lumber or even wooden vegetable crates. Glades hunters modeled these boats after Seminole canoes, though many rural white families

Passageway through the mangroves. Photograph by Deborah Mitchell.

bought and used Seminole canoes instead of making their own boats. A skiff's maneuverability came from being fairly lightweight and narrow, usually about two feet wide. At the same time, skiffs had to be long enough to accommodate the gear and provisions (sometimes for two men) needed on multiweek trips in the backcountry, and so they were generally sixteen to eighteen feet long. Necessities included mosquito netting (called "skeeter bars"), a ground cover, rifles, ammunition, tobacco, a pocketknife, a machete or ax, heavy bags of salt for preparing hides, coffee, a little meat (usually cooked down and stored in lard), matches, cooking grease, and if room allowed, some freshwater. Supplies that had to be kept dry, such as ammunition, were packed in "lard-can suitcases," five-gallon tin containers that were purchased or foraged from in-town grocery stores; these "suitcases" were balanced in the middle of the skiff.

Like the pirogues used in the Louisiana bayou, glade skiffs are pushed along using a long boat pole. Standing toward the back of the boat, the poler was elevated above the glade plane and from this position was able to watch the marsh's bottom for signs of game and to monitor changes in the surrounding landscape. Optimally, the skiff's wedge-shaped bow was formed by the intersection of two cypress boards, a design that allowed the poler to part the vegetation and glide over the thick grassy Everglades waters. A five-inch lift built into the skiff's stern prevented the bow from slapping against the water as the boat moved forward. This design made movement virtually silent. The stern's updraft also allowed the boat to be poled stern-first, granting greater maneuverability when turning around in narrow passages proved impracticable. The skiff's flat bottom allowed hunters to travel across miles of shallow marshes where the water was often only inches deep. Even with these design considerations, skillful poling was an "absolute" necessity for traveling in the Everglades, according to Everglades explorer Hugh Willoughby, as the shallow waters and thick grasses meant skiffs often had to be shoved along.[27]

Glen Simmons, talking about hunting with a friend, Lige Powers, evoked the difficulties of skiff trips:

> Lige had a way of easing a mean situation. Everything seemed to go against us on some of our long trips poling through the mangroves in a glades boat. The skeeters would be bad; it would be hot, rainy; the smudge bucket was always contrary; and the drinking water rotten. There are many blind cuts in the mangroves and sometimes after cutting, pulling, and poling for over an hour, the run would peter out, and you knew you had to dead-head back out. Nothing to do but growl and get with it. Lige might laugh and ask, "How about a little smile?" It helped.[28]

During the rainy season, forty-three species of Everglades mosquitoes form an unrelenting presence in the backcountry. Of these, the salt marsh mosquito is the most abundant and lays about 10,000 eggs per square foot in the exposed moist soils of the coastal marshes and mangrove swamps. On the inland hammocks or in the mangrove country, mosquitoes can be unbearable, so thick at times that you breathe them in. To combat mosquitoes,

Mr. and Mrs. R. M. Cox and child, with Ethel and Wilhelmina Kern, in a Seminole dugout canoe at Brown's Boat Landing, a trading post in the Big Cypress Swamp. Photograph by Julian Dimock, 1910; printed by permission of the American Museum of Natural History

skiffers burnt damp black mangrove wood in smudge pots in their boats. Although the smoke kept the mosquitoes at bay, it was acrid and pervasive, burning skiffers' eyes, yellowing their clothes, and clinging to their hair and skin. For glades hunters, mobility was clouded in a mist of strong-smelling smoke.

Even with the difficulties of skiff travel, as Simmons described, glades hunters covered many miles a day in their boats. The routes they used were hardly arbitrary. Instead, skiffers poled their boats through established passageways that formed tunnels through the mangrove jungles and snaked across the inland marshes. In some respects these skiff passages were akin to a watery system of routes similar to the network of roads in any town or village. In fact, at places these skiff routes crossed actual roadways, providing hunters with easy access to the backcountry. These intersections, called "jumping-off spots" or "landings," were marked by subtle variations in the landscape (a solitary palm, for instance), though to outsiders, including game wardens, landings remained largely invisible and unnoticed.

Many of these passageways followed the natural flows of water in the Everglades. For instance, the Shark and Taylor sloughs direct the flow of water within the southern Everglades, serving as primary connective features linking the northern and inland glades to the exterior mangrove swamps and Florida Bay. These sloughs meander about, widening and narrowing, and are intersected by numerous small creeks and waterways. Skiff routes across the landscape overlay these ecological features of the Everglades. For instance, one skiff route, now within Everglades National Park, followed the deeper channel of the Taylor Slough, continued on through the Taylor Creek, one of the slough's primary outlets, and ended at Little Madeira Bay.

The courses and intersections of these routes produced a conversation of sorts across the landscape. Routes, and the landings that marked the passageways, were often named after the person who "claimed" them. For instance, Ed Brooker's Landing at Whiskey Creek off the Old Ingraham Highway (now within Everglades National Park) was named for an old-timer who lived almost permanently at a camp a bit back from the landing. Brooker was a mythic figure in the glades. It appears that he moved into the southern Everglades in 1904, after hunting otter and plume birds around Lake Okeechobee. Before moving into the backcountry, he had been a fairly solid citizen, working as a railroad agent, owning a store, and homesteading large parcels of property. Reputedly because of a drinking problem, he gave up town life around 1916 and moved to a remote island in the backcountry, staying at his camp almost full-time during the Depression years. He farmed the island he lived on — clearing the center of the hammock, planting beans and tomatoes.

In part, these routes index territorial rights and community histories associated with those rights. For instance, to reach Brooker's camp from his landing, glades hunters traveled "maybe a half mile of crooks and turns" through narrow mangrove passageways. Yet other routes, described aptly as "tunnels," branched out from there and led to other routes, camps, and hunting territories. The rhizomic network radiating from Brooker's camp demarcated a region Brooker claimed as his own, and he kept the routes of the network cleared for easier passage. Other hunters were well aware of this territorialization. For instance, Lige Powers, another local hunter, kept his skiff hidden off the road near Brooker's Landing. When heading into the backcountry to hunt, Powers would "jump off" from Brooker's Landing, travel one of the passageways radiating from Brooker's camp, and then head off into other territories. Even if Powers or others did not come across Brooker in person, they moved through *his* territory. As they moved, they recalled stories about Brooker—his drinking provided endless fodder for stories both tragic and colorful.

If we understand, as Simon Schama has argued, landscapes as human geographies whose "scenery is built up as much from the strata of memory as from layers of rock,"[29] then the hunters' movements through gladeland passages open up these strata, like a coring machine digging deep into layers of memory and experience. Moving through the landscape created a kind of conversation about place as various camps, passages, and territorial demarcations were encountered. Hunters' journeys through the Everglades were not simply acts of "reading" the landscape, as if the landscape was a static text. Instead, reconfigured landscapes emerge as "communally-significant sites were encountered anew and subsequently viewed through the lens of altered events, times and personal experience."[30]

MOBILE LANDSCAPES

In his ethnography of the Paris Metro, Marc Augé refers to the Metro map as a "memory machine," arguing that each stop highlighted on the map indexes and generates individual and shared histories of place.[31] Like the Paris Metro, gladeland passageways, such as the Reef or Whiskey Creek, were shared within this community, forming a communally understood navigational network within a landscape that remained largely unmapped until the late 1950s. As with travel along the various stops and stations along the Paris Metro, the significance of glades hunters' journeys through anonymous thickets of saw grass or tropical hammocks lay in their reverberations with past events, real and imagined. Day after day, week after week, these men traveled across the Everglades, usually alone. Yet even in all this aloneness, amid hundreds of miles of isolated swamps, their discursive engagement, that *to and fro,* created and reinforced a sense of togetherness — or discourses of place, community, and common history. We might understand these spatial practices as strategies of territorialization. Yet this claiming only goes so far before the landscape itself offers its countermove — for the Everglades is a landscape that is in constant motion, a highly mobile landscape that resists the human world's efforts at staking claims. This is particularly true in the mangrove country.

R. mangle, or the red mangrove, has roots that snake in all directions and extend as far as two meters from the tree's trunk. This root multiplicity can elongate as much as nine millimeters per day.[32] Even if mangroves do not "build land" as the early literature suggested,[33] they participate in the building process.[34] *R. mangle's* stilting, looping network of roots grows in every direction, intersecting with neighboring trees to form "an almost impenetrable tangle."[35] This assemblage traps sediments in slow-moving water, which, in turn, accumulates to stabilize emerging landscapes. All of this growing — up and out and intertwining — made skiff passageways transitory.

While a boat's way is its progress and velocity, the glades' way had more to do with "making way," or the removal of obstacles to passage, than with the continuous progress of craft through water. Skiffers regularly poled their boats through narrow channels for days on end, an activity that typically involved hacking and shoving through walls of mangrove as well as fighting the wind and currents in open waters. On the more infrequently traveled routes, glades hunters often resorted to lying down in their skiffs and manhandling their way under and through the mangrove forests. Creeks were often plugged with fallen logs, requiring skiffers to repeatedly jump overboard and drag them aside or lift the boat over the debris. In these tough passageways, traveling a half mile took hours.

Each trip into the mangrove country entailed the rediscovery and redefinition of these passageways. At the turn of the last century, the ornithologist Frank Chapman described the mangrove forests of the Everglades: "The branches form a dense canopy overhead, and marks of the axe showed they had grown freely below, in places, limbs and roots having been cut out every yard of the way."[36] As Chapman suggests, moving through the passages in the mangroves involved hacking through the forests' confusing assemblage of roots and branches—even as the mangroves continued to grow back into new formations. To extend Augé's analogy of the Paris Metro, the tracks of the Everglades memory machine are in a state of continuous derailment. Imagine not clearly defined passages but, instead, networks of reconfiguration and rupture.

The metaphor of the mangrove guides my theoretical argument and the structure of this book. Although mangroves are trees, they are highly mobile and rhizomic. These properties allow us to resist the connotations of stability and order generally associated with the metaphor of a tree. Instead, thinking-as-mangroves helps us map the movements of people, animals, water, nutrients, sediment, and plant life in the Everglades. The mangrove, or *R. mangle,* connects, as Deleuze and Guattari have demonstrated, "semiotic chains of every nature . . . to very diverse modes of coding (biological, economic, etc.) that bring into play not only differing regimes of signs but also states of things of differing status."[37] In this chapter, hunters, mangroves, alligators, and fantastic snakes all are mobile, and their mobilities intersect. What I have sought to show in this chapter is that mobility is a strategy for claiming territory. In the territorial assemblage that is the hunter's landscape, both humans and nonhumans stake claims through their movements and resist counterclaims.

The Gang Vanishes into the Mysterious Swamp

Out of the somber stillness of the Everglades comes this story of John Ashley, bank-robber, highwayman, pirate, hi-jacker and murderer. Out of its labyrinthine maze of gnarled and twisted mangrove came John Ashley in his teens, heavily laden with otter and other furs that found a ready market and brought the necessities of life to a typical "cracker" family.

−HIX C. STUART, *The Notorious Ashley Gang:*
A Saga of the King and Queen of the Everglades

Though a jury convicted John Ashley for the murder of DeSoto Tiger and sentenced him to death by hanging, Ashley was never imprisoned for the crime. For reasons that remain unclear to me, Florida's Supreme Court reversed the jury's decision. With understandable frustration, local prosecutors then tried Ashley for bank robbery. In 1916 he was convicted of this lesser crime and sentenced to serve seventeen and one-half years at the notorious Raiford Prison in northern Florida. This was a time when prisoners in Florida labored on chain gangs or were leased to work in phosphate mines or turpentine camps. Ashley ended up serving only two years of his sentence at Raiford before being transferred to one such off-site work camp. After his transfer, Ashley and another inmate quickly escaped and fled southward to the Everglades. There, Laura Upthegrove waited.

O. B. Padgett, who was deputy sheriff for Palm Beach County at this time, described the region's mangrove forests and scrub hammocks as "alive with moonshine stills."[1] With plenty of freshwater and wood available to run the steam-powered stills, this was an ideal landscape for making illegal alcohol. It also was an ideal landscape for concealing a fugitive. Ashley remained at large for three years, operating moonshine stills throughout Palm Beach County. He was eventually arrested in Wauchula, Florida, as he tried to deliver a load of liquor to a garage. Until a fellow prisoner tipped them off, the arresting officers did not immediately know they had a wanted fugitive in their small jail. When his identity was confirmed, Ashley was returned to Raiford to serve out the remainder of his sentence. Incredibly, prison authorities once again transferred Ashley to the convict road crew, and, once again, he escaped and returned to the Everglades.

But it was not just John Ashley who escaped from confinement. It seems as if one posse or another, with or without dog teams, was always pursuing various gang members. For instance, like John Ashley, Ray Lynn and Clarence Middleton escaped from a prison road crew in Marianna, Florida. A couple years later, Hanford Mobley and another gang member forced open a skylight in their cell in the Broward County jail (where they had been transferred because of its higher security) and then used their blankets to lower themselves from the roof. These escapes were quickly followed by an excruciating repetition of roadblocks, stakeouts, and car chases.

Even after years of reading about the Ashley Gang, I am still surprised at the mundane ease of these escapes. A case in point: when John Ashley ran away from the Dade County jail, the guard pursued him on a bicycle. By anyone's accounting, the members of the gang proved themselves to be extremely dangerous. And yet they were not exactly criminal masterminds. Their escapes (and crimes too, for that matter) could hardly be characterized as meticulously planned. Even so, they seemed to repeatedly elude their captors. The Ashley Gang stories offer a simple explanation for this state of affairs. The explanation is not, as one might suppose, that the jails were understaffed or that local people were not particularly enthusiastic about capturing the gang or even that the enforcement technologies of the day (Model T Fords, telegrams, chicken wire, and the like) were unsophisticated. Instead, the Everglades is central to these explanations.

In the stories of the Ashley Gang, the Everglades is more than mere backdrop. There is a sense in these stories that the Ashley Gang was somehow a *product* of the Everglades — as if the Everglades gave birth to a sort of culture of transgression. Like the landscape's fantastic snakes and ferocious alligators, John Ashley appears to have emerged from the swamp's primordial abyss a fully formed criminal. It is this myth of origin that accounts, according to the stories, for the gang's ability to vanish, at will, into the landscape's inscrutable recesses. Ironically, the Everglades has held on to the Ashley Gang, allowing it to remain visible while so much else of the landscape's human history has vanished from our memories.

5. SEARCHING FOR PARADISE IN
THE FLORIDA EVERGLADES

So far in this book I have shown how in the hunter's landscape the human and nonhuman worlds are entangled, like a rhizome that is on the move. Enormous snakes lurk in mangrove jungles that are constantly growing and changing even as hunters hack their way through their enclosing roots and branches. While this territorial assemblage is not grounded or fixed, the trajectories I have explored so far have been localized, or at least swamp-specific. But of course there are agents of change (sea level rise, development schemes, federal and state water policies, animal rights activists) that stake their claims from locales far beyond the swamp's confines.

I use the phrase "the politics of nature" to describe the work of these broader agents of change. Following Bruno Latour, I understand "politics" as activities undertaken by collectives of humans and nonhumans. These collectives have histories and engage in processes of socialization and naturalization and, therefore, are political in the broadest sense.[1] Since the beginning of statehood, numerous agents have reshaped the Everglades landscape and altered the practices of humans and nonhumans. Most notably, this politics of nature has pivoted around the seemingly contradictory impulses to develop the Everglades and conserve it from development. In this chapter I explore the ways in which some of the first scientists to appreciate the Everglades contributed to conservation efforts. Further, we see how this scientific appreciation becomes a specific kind of politics, what we might call the politics of naturalization, which entails a kind of selective vision that is blind to nature's humanity. Here, I look closely at how the politics of naturalization have transformed a particular site now within Everglades National Park, Royal

Royal palms along the eastern side
of Royal Palm Hammock, 1916.
Photograph by John Kunkel Small;
courtesy of the State Archives of Florida.

Palm Hammock, from a hunter's landscape into a "natural landscape," or a landscape where the territorial claims of hunters are highly circumscribed.

Parts of the world become recognized, valued, known, or "famous," for want of a better word, based on their perceived ecological significance. These landscapes go by many names: "hotspots" of biodiversity, habitats for endangered species, or even "buffer zones," a term given to lands that serve as barriers between critical ecological habitats, such as watersheds, and adjacent development.[2] Some landscapes, such as the one I am writing about here, gain mythical status for the role they have played within the field of natural history. These are geographies where ecological discoveries occurred or where fieldwork and scholarship led to larger disciplinary shifts in ecological theory or method. For instance, Wisconsin's sand counties are inextricably linked to Aldo Leopold's approach to wildlife conservation and environmental ethics.[3] Of course, many such landscapes do not acquire the national, and even international, reputation of Leopold's sand counties. Instead, their resonance is limited to scholars specializing in the natural history and ecology of specific regions. Royal Palm Hammock, now within Everglades National Park, is one such locale. This chapter offers an account of Royal Palm Hammock's rise to fame, and more particularly, I detail the politics of that ascension. In doing so I demonstrate how ecological fame-making is a politics of nature that requires the cooperation of humans (visiting naturalists, local hunters, funding agencies, and others) and nonhumans (royal palm trees, for example).

Thousands upon thousands of tree islands punctuate the vast open marshes and prairies of southern Florida's Everglades. These tree islands are classified by the dominant types of vegetation found on them, generally either wetland species or tropical hardwoods. Although wetland tree islands exist throughout the southeastern United States (the cypress swamps of the Okefenokee Swamp, for example), tropical hardwood islands, called hammocks, occur exclusively in the southern Everglades (from about Miami southward). The term "hammock" has an unclear origin, perhaps originating in the Seminole word for "home," although the Spanish *hamaca*, from the Arawakan indigenous word for "fish nets," dates to the mid-sixteenth century, and "hummock," also dating from the mid-sixteenth century, is a nautical term used to describe a small hill along a seacoast. Regardless of etymology,

Location of Royal Palm Hammock (also called Paradise Key) in the Florida Everglades.

hammocks as habitat are unique to southern Florida, and Royal Palm Hammock is, by far, the most famous hammock in the Everglades.[4]

Today, Royal Palm, which is about a mile long and a half mile wide, is the most visited site within Everglades National Park. The Gumbo Limbo Trail provides access to Royal Palm's understory. As you enter the hammock, the bright heat of a Florida day abruptly gives way, as if you had walked into a darkened, damp closet. There is an immediate sense of closeness, as the vegetation is dense and disorderly and the air is heavy with that musty richness particular to the tropics. The trees within Everglades hammocks are the same species found throughout the West Indian region of the American tropics, including cabbage palm, wild tamarind, West Indian mahogany, pigeon plum, lancewood, poisonwood, wild coffee, white stoppers, and gumbo limbo, also called the tourist tree for its red, peeling bark. Particular hammocks, including Royal Palm, are famed for their abundant bromeliads, delicate and rare orchids, and fanciful banded tree snails — making them targets for collectors of all kinds.[5]

To understand how Royal Palm acquired its status as a landscape of ecological significance, so significant in fact that it became the cornerstone of efforts to create a national park, I have analyzed the accounts of fieldwork that established and detailed the site's importance to the broader scientific community. This literature, spanning from the late 1800s through the mid-1930s, includes scientific reports — many of which were supported by the Smithsonian Institution and other critical research institutions of the era — letters, field notes and photographs collected in archives, bibliographies of key naturalists, newspaper articles, and other published accounts of fieldwork in the Everglades. Though I have analyzed the research of numerous naturalists, the key figures in this chapter are John Kunkle Small, botanist and curator for the New York Botanical Garden; Charles Torrey Simpson, a conchologist locally considered the "John Muir" of the Everglades; and Hugh Willoughby, a gentlemen explorer and surveyor who was the first person to publish an account of crossing the Everglades from west to east. At the turn of the last century, this literature, particularly the work of Small and Simpson, was critical to efforts to protect and conserve Royal Palm.[6] In addition, these early surveys and accounts of Royal Palm's biota continue to be important to biophysical scientists examining ecological change in the Everglades.

In the official national park literature that discusses the significance of Royal Palm, scant attention goes to any human history of the hammock; instead, the site's ecological worth and rarity are emphasized.[7] Though the visitor's experience of Royal Palm excludes indications of the site's human life, it was once a key location for local peoples engaged in a variety of productive and reproductive activities. It served as a central node in the hunter's landscape. This neglect of the site's human history will come as no surprise to readers familiar with the literature documenting the dispossession of peoples from national parks and protected areas. Roderick Neumann refers to the particular vision of nature that presupposed and supported these dispossessions as the "national park ideal," a Euro-American aesthetics of Edenic, uninhabited wilderness.[8] Similarly, Mark Spence's work has shown how the national park ideal relies upon an "atemporal *natural* history" that effectively erases the human history of landscapes, such as those that would become Yosemite, Glacier, and Yellowstone national parks.[9]

As this literature details, the history of the national park ideal in the United States is both simultaneous with and contingent upon the encroachment of white settlers on traditional indigenous lands, as well as the genocides that made these dispossessions possible. The Everglades is no exception to this colonialist history. White settlement in southern Florida was only feasible after decades of war with the Seminoles. To escape Andrew Jackson's brutal campaign of removal, the Seminoles sought refuge and independence within ever-more-remote areas of the southern Everglades. By the Second Seminole War (1835–1842), Seminoles were certainly living in and around Royal Palm. For instance, a few years after the war, Jack Jackson, who surveyed the southern Everglades in 1848, camped three miles from Royal Palm and referred to this region as the "Indian Hunting Grounds," suggesting that Seminoles were still living in the area at that time.[10] Understanding this historical legacy and the ongoing colonialist rhetorics that frame contemporary relations and disputes over boundaries and usage between Everglades indigenous peoples and the national park is of critical importance, and its account has yet to be written.

The period I examine here is one in which white rural and Seminole peoples were engaged in similar hunting and trade practices, in many cases using the same landscapes for these activities, including Royal Palm Hammock. This chapter explores the intersections of these histories at Royal Palm and their distinct roles in the coproduction of ecological knowledge about the site. I pay particular attention to the mechanisms that displaced from the landscape rural white people, a community fairly marginalized from the emerging metropolis of Miami to the north. As I discuss later in this section, naturalists constructed indigenous and rural white relationships to landscapes in starkly different terms. This chapter focuses on the particular conceptual space that white gladesmen were assigned in the formation of Royal Palm's scientific value.

The parents and grandparents of the people I have interviewed for my fieldwork did not leave written accounts of their experiences in the Everglades. To gain some insight into this earlier period, I began reading the only available literature of that time, the early natural history, hoping to gain a glimpse of glades life through the eyes of visiting scientists. Their field notes and reports are ambiguous texts at best, and a narrative form that borrows heavily from the era's adventure-travel writing. Both genres offer similar constructions of locals: careless rubes, alcoholics, equally infantile and dangerous, with "local color" serving as a mechanism to claim authority over landscapes both inhabited and strangely beyond the pale of civilization. Here I piece together the spare clues of local collaboration in science making at Royal Palm found in these naturalists' accounts, while at the same time using oral histories of the hammock to reframe and problematize their narratives. Doing so offers evidence of how Royal Palm's natural history, as a specific way of seeing the landscape, articulates with the site's human history.

Science is often portrayed as a sort of handmaiden to state conservation movements, as a mechanism to justify the control or removal of peoples from lands deemed environmentally sensitive. Yet as Bruce Braun has demonstrated, not only are scientific discourses *instrumental* to the dispossession of locals from landscapes, but they also constitute nature and culture as knowable in particular kinds of ways. To illustrate his point, Braun analyzed the fieldwork of George Mercer Dawson, who conducted fieldwork for the U.S. Geological Survey during the 1870s in British Columbia. In his field notes and reports, Dawson meticulously detailed *both* the Haida culture and the landscapes he encountered, yet his narratives contain striking bifurcations, treating Native culture and the landscape as if they were unrelated categories of the world. Braun convincingly demonstrated that this demarcation abstracts Native peoples from the lived experience of their worlds. The fieldwork of Dawson and others did not ignore Native presence; instead, these landscape epistemologies made people and nature legible as unrelated orders of knowledge. Braun argued that contemporary land management approaches that treat Native peoples as merely another stakeholder are shaped by these earlier ways of seeing the world.[11]

Yet at the same time, as I show here, naturalists treated indigenous peoples as somehow within the same romanticized conceptual space as landscapes they considered wilderness. Natural history surveys, like natural history museums, often included an enumeration of indigenous peoples and their culture, typically as if they were one of the notable curiosities of the landscape.[12] For instance, W. E. Safford, an economic botanist with the U.S. Department of Agriculture, conducted a survey of Royal Palm during September 1917. His comprehensive study covered "all branches of natural history" and included chapters detailing the hammock's trees, epiphytes, mollusks, spiders, insects, fishes, reptiles, birds, and, finally, aboriginal Indians and their successors, the Seminoles. This last section catalogs the "fine physique" and culture of the Tequesta and Calusa peoples, information primarily derived from Spanish colonial accounts, as well as the use of native plants by the contemporary indigenous peoples.[13]

Though certainly problematically, naturalists considered indigenous peoples as somehow *of the landscape,* spatially naturalized within particular biota and geomorphology — this metonymic association arising, no doubt, from earlier debates concerning the singular or multiple origins of racial types. On the other hand, naturalists' constructions of nonindigenous peoples were substantially different. Not only were Euro-American inhabitants of wilderness abstracted from nature, but they were also constituted as *out of place.* This was certainly the case at Royal Palm, which was not only a landscape devoid of humanity but a landscape naturalists considered under siege by rural whites.

The central argument of this chapter is that becoming ecologically famous, and thus worthy of protection, required the transformation of Royal Palm Hammock into a "smooth object," Latour's term for ontologies devoid of their inherent material and ideological conflicts, incongruities, and biosocial entanglements.[14] Smoothing out Royal Palm required the "generification" of the site's ecology and its peoples into intelligible, stable, and generalizable categories of the world.[15] For naturalists, Royal Palm came to represent a singular example of the tropics within the continental United States. Its ecological value lay in its exotic and pristine *tropicality,* a generalized taxon that was considered particularly worthy of investigation and protection. Similarly, naturalists portrayed the rural whites living in and relying upon this tropical exemplar as nonendemic invaders. This form of generification required a monocular vision that ignored the diversities of the hammock's social nature. First, naturalists simply did not see, or did not acknowledge, the intimate connections rural whites had to the site, including ample evidence of long-term and multiple strategies of production and reproduction. Second, what naturalists did see corresponded to their sense that all white presence within the Everglades was equally detrimental; they made no distinction between the people who had been living within the Everglades for a century and the mass of recent arrivals settling and transforming southern Florida at that time. Third, although both rural white hunters and Seminole people were fundamental to the fieldwork that established Royal Palm's scientific worth — literature that was directly used to justify the hammock's protection as a state park and later a national park — naturalists discounted local ways of knowing the landscape by portraying these epistemologies as rudimentary and intuitive.

What follows is an account of the complex material and discursive relationships among naturalists, white local peoples, and the construction of Royal Palm's scientific significance, focusing on the late nineteenth and early twentieth centuries. I start by examining one of the first visits to the hammock by a nonlocal, Hugh Willoughby, who conducted a survey in the southern Everglades in 1897. In the next section, I examine the history of fieldwork at Royal Palm and explore how the quest to discover unique and rare biota determined the specific ways in which the hammock became ecologically significant to the naturalist community. In *All Creatures: Naturalists, Collectors, and Biodiversity, 1850–1950*, Robert Kohler provides a compelling study of the transformations in American cultural values and infrastructure that prefigured and supported natural history research at the beginning of the last century.[16] Due to the scale of Kohler's project, his portrayal of local nonspecialists in natural history fieldwork stems primarily from naturalists' accounts. By incorporating ethnographic and other sources, I provide a more nuanced understanding of the social relations of scientific production. As a counterpoint to naturalists' representations of Royal Palm's natural history, the third section details the hammock's human life, which is considerably circumscribed in the naturalists' accounts. In the final section, I draw on Latour's notion of the "smooth object" to describe the production of natural history discourses.[17] This smoothing out, I argue, entails the generification of the site's social nature, a representation that ultimately shapes contemporary understandings of the human history of the Everglades as singularly threatening.

DISCOVERING PARADISE

Southern Florida's naturalist community first became aware of Royal Palm Hammock in the late nineteenth century, though it was not until the early years of the next century that these scholars began to publish detailed descriptions and surveys of the hammock's flora, fauna, and geomorphology. One of the greatest obstacles to conducting fieldwork in the southern Everglades was the landscape's perceived inaccessibility and related problems of navigating an "unmapped" landscape.[18] Rendering the Everglades legible for field research required surveying the landscape. Several efforts to do so were undertaken between the late nineteenth century and the early decades of the twentieth century. Most notably, Hugh deLaussett Willoughby, of Newport, Rhode Island, conducted one of the earliest of these surveying efforts. His account, *Across the Everglades: A Canoe Journey of Exploration,* initially published in 1898, offers the first record of a westward passage across the Everglades and includes a description of a visit to Royal Palm. Willoughby, as befitting the narrative style of the era, described his Everglades exploration in terms that highlight the landscape's exoticism and hitherto unknown qualities, geographically situated within the poetics of colonial encounters:

> It may seem strange, in our days of Arctic and African exploration, for the general public to learn that in our very midst . . . we have a tract of land one hundred and thirty miles long and seventy miles wide that is as much unknown to the white man as the heart of Africa.[19]

As Willoughby's goal was to establish an accurate surveying transect across this unknown landscape, he prepared for his trip with rigor, spending a year attending to the details of navigational equipment, boat rigging, and appropriate clothing. His serendipitous encounter with a local hunter named Ed Brewer, whom he "accidentally met" while in the then frontier town of Miami, proved fortuitous. Here and there, other narratives briefly mentioned Brewer, and these accounts coalesce to form an incomplete sketch of the man's biography. Willoughby's descriptions of Brewer are ethnologi-cal in tone and are worth repeating:

> He was a man of medium height, heavily built without being fat, black hair, black eyes, inured to hardship, and able to make himself comfortable in his long tramps, with a canoe, a tin pot, a blanket, a deer-skin, a mosquito-bar, and a rifle, with perhaps a plug or two of tobacco as a luxury.[20]

According to Willoughby, Brewer was born in Virginia, although he had lived in the southern Everglades for many years supporting himself as a hunter and trapper. Local gossip suggested the man's character was ques-tionable, and in fact Willoughby's friends warned against hiring him.[21]

Several years later, another local guide told Anthony W. Dimock, a travel and adventure writer, that a shoot-out with a disreputable neighbor had forced Brewer to relocate from the Ten Thousand Islands, on the west coast of the Everglades, to Miami.[22] C. S. "Ted" Smallwood, in his memoir of pioneer-ing life on Chokoloskee Island during the late 1800s, mentioned in passing that Brewer was known for trading with area Seminoles at their backcountry camps. Smallwood said that Brewer would leave with a canoe loaded down with liquor and calico and return from the glades with money and skins. He was also a man who enjoyed playing the fiddle for small gatherings.[23] Whatever Brewer's character, his knowledge of the Everglades backcountry and expertise seems to have been locally well established. For instance, six months prior to guiding Willoughby, Brewer had led a three-day hunting and exploration trip into the Everglades for a party that included a local judge, a point that would suggest that whatever Brewer's reputation, his dis-tinction as a guide outweighed any concerns by his clients for their personal safety at his hands.[24]

Willoughby had never camped in the Everglades before, so for over a month Brewer tutored Willoughby in what could and could not be eaten, hunted and fished for their food, located dry sites for making camp, and hauled a burdensome amount of surveying equipment and other supplies across the Everglades in a canvas-covered canoe. Willoughby appreciated Brewer's attentions:

I always found him brave and industrious, constantly denying himself, deceiving me as to his appetite when our supplies ran low that I might be more comfortable, and many a night did he stay up an extra hour while I was finishing my notes and plotting work, that he might tuck me in my cheese cloth from the outside.[25]

While Brewer's role of caretaker in this journey is clear and appreciated in Willoughby's account, the reader's sense of Brewer's expertise as a guide remains more elusive. Willoughby's endless narrative of sextant readings, surveying stations, and longitudinal and latitudinal points convey and establish his techno-expertise, certainly contributing to the account's ongoing legitimacy. Yet evidence from other sources suggests that Brewer also had considerable knowledge of the famously difficult Everglades terrain, reportedly spending periods of up to six months in the backcountry at a time. It also seems that he had traveled on at least half of Willoughby's route previously. For instance, Brewer claimed squatters' rights on an island full of towering palms at the southern end of Long Pine Key, a series of inland islands that served as an important designation and reference point throughout Willoughby's journey.[26] This island later became known as Royal Palm Hammock.

We can only guess at what each man learned from the other on their trip across the Everglades. Judging from the subsequent accounts and literature on the historic Everglades, Brewer's claims to Royal Palm Hammock and his considerable knowledge of the landscape do not become a part of the concordance contributing to Royal Palm Hammock's fame. Aside from his explorations in the Everglades, Willoughby is remembered as a famous aviator, as a colleague and friend to other famous aviators, including Orville Wright, and as a founder of the Rhode Island Naval Reserve. No doubt his social connections also contributed to his account's popularity. Willoughby's book was certainly successful; it was reprinted in several editions and was reviewed in prestigious journals, including the *Geographical Journal* of the Royal Geographical Society and the *Journal of the American Geographical Society of New York*. Although Willoughby's exploration brought attention to the Everglades landscape, including the attention of naturalists, Royal

Palm's history of fieldwork reveals how the quest to discover unique and rare biota determined the specific ways in which the hammock became ecologically valued.

THE LANDSCAPE'S MYSTERIOUS MAGIC

Royal Palm's rarity lay in its towering stand of royal palm trees, as the name suggests. Yet although these palms brought the hammock to the naturalist community's immediate attention, the hammock's real (and exotic) appeal lay in its status as a rare exemplar of the "tropics" within the continental United States. Vladimir Nabokov, discussing the production of scientific knowledge, said that some landscapes have a kind of "mysterious magic" that propels naturalists to discover new species and the unknown qualities of nature.[27] Nabokov, with his well-known obsession with butterfly taxonomy and collecting, would have found a kindred spirit in Charles Torrey Simpson, the most famous early Everglades naturalist. Simpson, a conchologist by specialization, reportedly could identify 10,000 shells by sight, giving each its correct Latin nomenclature.[28] In terms similar to Nabokov's, Simpson described his own deep connection to the process of fieldwork:

> I do not want to investigate nature as though I were solving a problem in mathematics. . . . In my attempts to unravel its mysteries I have a sense of reverence and devotion, I feel as though I were on enchanted ground. And whenever any of its mysteries are revealed to me I have a feeling of elation . . . just as though the birds or the trees had told me their secrets and I had understood their language.[29]

Royal Palm's mysterious magic offered naturalists a way of encountering and seeing the landscape through the prism of its unknown qualities and rarities. The practice of fieldwork became the method for translating the landscape's mysterious magic into disciplined knowledge.

John Kunkel Small, preeminent botanist and curator for the New York Botanical Garden, in his article "Royal Palm Hammock," offered a history of fieldwork at Royal Palm and reported on two "independent" discoveries of the hammock that occurred in the late 1800s.[30] Seminole people who were living and hunting in the area facilitated both these discoveries, a point suggesting that whatever rights Ed Brewer had to the island, other people were already occupying it, at least on and off, prior to his claim. In the first instance, Kirk Munroe, an early settler, author, and advocate for the Seminoles, recalled being guided in February 1882 to an Indian camp that was established "on the edge of a low hammock," where a number of royal palms grew.[31] This visit to the hammock took place during a four-month canoe trip that Munroe took along Florida's western coast. Two Seminole men asked Munroe to follow them back to their camp, a distance of twenty-five or thirty miles away, to aid an ill child. Tragically, by the time Munroe's party reached the camp, the child had died. Though Munroe only spent one evening at the Seminole camp, he was struck by the presence of a magnificent stand of royal palms. Munroe took particular note of the trees, as he had not encountered them elsewhere in the Everglades, though he recognized the species, having seen it previously while traveling in Panama. Years later, when writing to Small, Munroe was convinced that this Seminole camp was "Royal Palm Hammock," having sighted the hammock again on another trip in 1900.

The second "discovery" of the hammock, as reported by Small, provides a crucial link in the history of fieldwork at the site. In 1893, Francis M. and John J. Soar, nurserymen and amateur botanists who lived in the Little River settlement in what is now northern Miami, were told about a "large island, with many tall palms growing on it" by Seminoles camping near their home.[32] In their nursery business the Soars grew citrus for northern markets, later specializing in ornamentals propagated from native plants. Many of these plants were collected during botanical explorations with visiting naturalists.[33] To reach the hammock, the Soar brothers sailed southward along the eastern coast of Florida and up Black Point Creek until it ended where the "pinelands meet the everglade prairie." The brothers then walked about twenty miles along the prairie before sighting the aforementioned tall palms; to reach the hammock they waded six miles across the slough that borders the island.[34]

The presence of these mysterious and rare towering palms certainly impressed John Soar, as he later undertook this fairly difficult journey on at least two other occasions while guiding naturalists to the site. When naturalists were first conducting fieldwork at Royal Palm Hammock, they found approximately one hundred of these palms at the site, rising high above the rest of the hammock's vegetation. Clearly, the royal palms granted the hammock its initial distinction and struck even the most seasoned naturalist with considerable awe. Simpson, after describing the hammock's many properties, said, "But the glory, the matchless triumph of the great forest is the royal palms."[35] For these early naturalists, the palms lent the hammock nobility and charm, making the site the "most romantic hammock in the southern tip of the state."[36] The palms were like "arboreal monuments," signaling the hammock's botanical importance.[37] Most importantly, they were what made the hammock unique.[38]

Today, within the discourse of contemporary ecological claims making, the presence of a single rare species, for instance the infamous spotted owl, justifies the ecological territorialization of landscapes. In the case of Royal Palm, the literature suggests that these naturalists felt the need to establish the landscape's ecological worth beyond the mere presence of these exceptional trees. To authenticate Royal Palm's overall ecological importance required repeated surveys of the hammock, which taken together form a genealogy of field research and, importantly, a replicable record. The Soar brothers must have told Small about Royal Palm, for Small, who knew the Soars, appears to have been the first institutionally supported scientist to conduct research at the site, which he did in 1903.[39] A few months later, John Soar, who was Simpson's neighbor, guided Simpson and Alvah Augustus Eaton, a fern specialist, to the hammock.[40] On this trip, the men drove the "preposterous" roads from Miami into the glades, stopped at a camp once used by surveyors, then trudged on foot the last three miles to the hammock. Simpson described the walk through the rocky glades as consisting "mostly in slipping down and getting up again," oftentimes while wading through water up to their armpits. During the trip, Eaton was badly shaken after stepping on the tail of an alligator, mistakenly thinking it was a log, and Soar became terribly ill, a result, Simpson suggested, from the nauseating odor of a rattlesnake the party skinned for a specimen.[41]

In the years between the Soars' first visit in 1893 and the establishment of the Royal Palm State Park in 1916, at least twenty separate documented research expeditions were undertaken. The institutional affiliations and academic credentials of the scientists who conducted research at Royal Palm indicate the widespread interest in and the importance of the location in the naturalist community. For instance, in 1904, Nathan Lord Britton, director in chief of the New York Botanical Garden, visited the hammock, as did Roland Harper, one of ecology's early pioneers (though he was still a graduate student at Columbia University at the time), and Peter Henry Rolfs, then plant pathologist in charge of the U.S. Department of Agriculture's Sub-tropical Laboratory in Miami. A few years later, in 1908, fieldwork was conducted at the hammock by Ernst Bessey, well-regarded botanist and son of Charles Edwin Bessey (considered the father of modern botany), and the plant pathologist G. L. Fawcett. John C. Gifford, one of America's first professional foresters and a strong voice for swampland reclamation and for the protection of Royal Palm, visited the hammock in 1916. The following year, W. E. Safford of the U.S. Department of Agriculture produced one of the most comprehensive surveys of Royal Palm's biota and natural history. During this period, Small returned to Royal Palm on at least fifteen occasions, and Simpson also made repeated trips to the hammock. By 1916, researchers had documented 241 kinds of plants, including 162 native species. Safford not only exhaustively characterized the entirety of the hammock's natural history but deposited representative samples into collections at the Smithsonian Institution, the U.S. National Museum, the Bureau of Entomology, and the Bureau of Biological Survey.[42] Arthur Howell, ornithologist for the Bureau of Biological Survey and author of the seminal *Florida Bird Life,* produced a list of 128 species of birds spotted in or around the hammock, though he considered the hammock's birdlife "surprisingly meager."[43] By any measure, Royal Palm amassed a considerable record of fieldwork, particularly since the location spans only about four hundred acres.

More important, this baseline information allowed researchers to situate the hammock's characteristics and value in relation to other landscapes in the known world. The consensus demonstrated that the hammock both contained specimens "new to science" and represented a habitat "not before known to occur naturally in the United States."[44] That unknown habitat was the tropics. As David Arnold has argued, the determination of *tropicality* becomes a way of defining landscapes as both "alien and distinctive" from European temperate climates, making them a kind of privileged locale for experiencing and studying nature.[45] The sense of wonder at discovering a tropical wilderness within the continental United States became a trope repeated throughout these accounts of early fieldwork. Safford described Royal Palm as "almost unique from a biological point of view, presenting as it does a remarkable example of subtropical jungle within the limits of the United States in which primeval conditions of animals and plant life remained unchanged by man."[46]

In effect, these naturalists treated the landscape as if it were a geographic extension of the tropics, comparing the location, at various times, to the West Indies, western Cuba, the Bahamas, Jamaica, and Puerto Rico, among other popular sites for tropical fieldwork. In doing so, their narratives incorporated their fieldwork into a broader disciplinary tradition of tropical natural history dating back to Alexander von Humbolt's travels in South and Central America at the turn of the nineteenth century.[47] During these early years of research at Royal Palm, the lure of the tropics certainly had not waned. For instance, in 1902, just one year before Small conducted his first survey of the hammock for the New York Botanical Garden, his supervisor, Nathan Lord Britton, began his thirty years of fieldwork on the tropical flora of Puerto Rico. Discursively reterritorializing the southern Florida landscape into the tropics invested the hammock with exotic allure, certainly increasing the hammock's visibility as a site for fieldwork, continued institutional interest, and, eventually, protection. Moreover, by ascribing tropicality to the hammock, naturalists were able to increase the site's legibility, fitting it within known categories of the world while at the same time arguing for its uniqueness.

This era of fieldwork at Royal Palm corresponds to what Robert Kohler has described as the "survey" period of American naturalist research.[48] Kohler's thorough analysis offers critically important insights into the broad transformations in American society, transformations that shaped the culture and practice of natural history survey work at the turn of the last century. One of Kohler's central arguments is that during this period, changes in American social values and practices toward wilderness, transportation networks, and mixed gradients of settled and undisturbed land uses brought many Americans into closer contact with "wilderness" landscapes. In effect, wilderness was essentially now in peoples' backyards.

This proximity resulted in new forms of residential knowledge about these "inner frontiers," Kohler's term for America's intermingled landscapes of

Royal palm, at Royal Palm Hammock. Photograph by John Kunkel Small, 1918; courtesy of the State Archives of Florida.

John Soar's truck stuck in mud near Royal Palm Hammock. Photograph by John Kunkel Small, 1915; courtesy of the State Archives of Florida

"densely inhabited and wild areas" of the era.[49] By examining naturalists' reports, field notes, and other archival material, Kohler demonstrated the critical importance of residential knowledge to the era's natural history survey work. Kohler uses the term "residential knowledge" to distinguish between particularistic and global forms of knowledge, with "residential knowledge" suggesting an experiential epistemology that "comes from living in a place"; it differs from the global (theory-producing) knowledge scientists practice.[50] Institutional and financial constraints limited the time field scientists had for their research. Residential knowledge, therefore, acted as a catalyst to the naturalists' knowledge of the inner frontier's specificities. In particular,

Kohler revealed the close connections and indebtedness field scientists had to "amateur" naturalists, such as members of bird-watching clubs. The practice of professional fieldwork, with its claims to scientific authority, transformed the amateur's residential knowledge into globalized, as Kohler described it, "cosmopolitan" scientific knowledge. On the other hand, professional naturalists found the residential knowledge of *other* locals, such as hunters or commercial harvesters, less reliable, and they often considered the assistance of these locals downright counterproductive. Kohler's interrogation of field scientists' accounts presents a portrait of *these* locals as at best questionable assistants and at worst untrustworthy drunks, not up to the demands of proper specimen preparation, and even as folks apt to steal the valuable specimens they were hired to collect. I have no doubt this message resonated in Kohler's sources.

Yet because of the broad scope of his investigation, Kohler leaves unexplored the social relations of this place-based knowledge production. One wonders how amateur naturalists first came to know the landscapes of the inner frontiers. How did this residential knowledge move up the chain of ever-more-authoritative command? A cartography of science should attend to the social relations of knowledge production, including the nuances of residential knowledge exchange. By focusing in on the mechanisms of knowledge production at specific places such as Royal Palm, I am able to trace the intersections and absences that characterize the social relations of place-based knowledge. Unnamed Seminoles brought Royal Palm to the attention of explorers such as Kirk Munroe and amateur naturalists such as the Soar brothers, who were interested in local botany and in propagating this flora for commercial purposes. The Soars then introduced the hammock to professional naturalists such as John Kunkel Small and Charles Torrey Simpson. Euro-American hunters, such as Ed Brewer and countless others, served as guides to the hammock and other regions of the Everglades backcountry. The published accounts resulting from these networks of relations alerted other naturalists to the site.

These networks of relations offer a clue into the process by which residential knowledge became transformed into scientific knowledge of Royal Palm. My own fieldwork with glades hunters who served as guides to visiting naturalists suggests that the motivations cementing these relationships were highly variable. Some guides assisted solely for the money and were often skeptical of naturalists' abilities to "know" the landscape as they did in such a short time. Others were motivated by friendships and a sense that they were contributing to important research. Some guides, particularly those working after the national park was established, used these field trips to survey areas closed off to them, occasionally returning to those sites for clandestine hunting. These varied and overlapping motivations surely shaped locals' relationships with naturalists and affected the coproduction of knowledge then and now. We can only surmise the motivations and related power dynamics that informed Royal Palm's fieldwork history. What is clearer is that the landscape's mysterious magic, the lens for viewing Royal Palm's rarities, was decidedly monocular, leaving much of the hammock's life only partially visible.

THE SOCIAL LIFE OF HAMMOCKS

Seminole and Euro-American hunters employed similar hunting techniques, sold their hides and pelts to the same buyers, bought supplies — such as ammunition, guns, sewing machines, and dry goods — at the same trading posts.[51] For both Seminole and Euro-American settlers, this hunting and foraging lifestyle required spending extended periods in the Everglades. Hunting parties stayed in the backcountry for weeks on end, walking and poling canoes or narrow skiffs across miles of open marsh and mangrove swamps. On these backcountry trips, hunters used hammocks as campsites. Depending on how good the hunting was in a particular area, hunters would stay at their camps for a few days to a couple of weeks.

My interviews with former alligator hunters indicate that Seminole and white settlers continued to hunt and camp on the hammocks in and around Royal Palm well into the 1930s, well after the hammock was designated a state park in 1916. In fact, hunting and trapping activities continued up to and after the establishment of the national park in 1947, particularly in accessible areas such as Royal Palm.[52] Stories abound of Prohibition-era moonshiners running whiskey stills throughout Royal Palm, taking advantage of the hammock's freshwater and slow-burning wood. During this same period, just outside the boundaries of the hammock, fairly large-scale truck farming took place, complete with on-site vegetable-packing facilities that drew a varied population. The slough that runs along Royal Palm, conventionally called Taylor Slough, was locally referred to as Dead-Pecker Slough, a reminder of the consequences of consorting with the prostitutes who hung out at the farm-labor camps. Clearly, local practices of production (and reproduction, if the stories of prostitution are true) required an intimate knowledge of the landscape.

This social history distorts the naturalists' narrative of an undiscovered and isolated hammock. Naturalists dealt with this contradiction by constructing local landscape practices as deviant to the site's ecological integrity, repeatedly portraying Euro-American presence at Royal Palm as being "out of place" and largely transgressive to nature's economy. In their descriptions of the site, and the Everglades more generally, naturalists make brief mention of the Seminoles—when human life is acknowledged at all. Their inclusion of the Seminoles in the conceptual space of the Everglades is hardly scholarly or thoughtful. Instead, the Seminoles serve as a metonym for the landscape's isolation. The Seminoles (nameless, stable categories of difference) belong to the landscape and help establish Royal Palm as a remote tropical Paradise awaiting discovery. For example, Small attributed the late discovery of royal palms in Florida to the fact that "parts of the Florida peninsula [have] not been penetrated by the white man."[53] Similarly, the materials advertising Willoughby's famous journey portray the Everglades as a Seminole landscape where "no white man had ever traveled."[54] In some sense, the presence of the Seminoles, as a narrative trope, acts to preclude the emplacement of rural whites. Although the mechanics of this landscape racialization lie beyond the scope of this study, it serves as a strategy of scientific claims making and as a means of determining who belongs and who does not.

Yet the narrative effacement of rural whites from the site's natural history was far from complete. The restricted ways in which naturalists recognized this community speak to the mechanisms of smoothing out that ultimately cast rural whites' history aside. Concern over the hammock's future is a palpable refrain throughout early Everglades literature. For instance, Small, in an overview of his research in southern Florida during 1915, argued for the urgency of his fieldwork in the face of "exceedingly far-reaching and conspicuous changes taking place with the southward advance of civilization in the little known [region]."[55] A few years later, Simpson decried the changes that had taken place in the decades since he had first started his fieldwork in southern Florida: "I arraign our civilization before the bar of justice for its high crimes and misdemeanors in destroying all that is useful and beautiful which nature has so bounteously given us."[56] Again and again, the threat of environmental change disrupts the objective tone of this literature. Small, in particular, warned of the need to protect the hammock from locals. Specific transgressions Small detailed include intentions to clear the hammock for a future citrus grove and the introduction of exotic species.[57] Without a doubt, Royal Palm's social history does include episodes of local commodification of the landscape. For instance, in the same newspaper article that detailed Brewer's claim to squatter's rights on Royal Palm, the author mentioned that Brewer was at the time engaged (apparently unsuccessfully) in selling the hammock's towering palms.[58] Still, even considering this and other similar episodes, the naturalists' accounts present only a partial vision.

Though naturalists considered the practices of white gladesmen a threat to the ecological integrity of the site, they also depended upon local information, or residential knowledge, for the success of their fieldwork. Naturalists attended to this incongruity by constructing local landscape epistemologies as being distinctly inferior to knowledge gained through fieldwork. Small made a particular point of distinguishing between the kind of knowledge held by "hunters who penetrated the Everglades in search of the furs and skins of various native animals" and the information produced systematically through scientific exploration.[59] Even Simpson, who throughout his writings articulated his respect for the people he encountered during his fieldwork, characterized local understandings as distinctly unsophisticated: "The sight and other senses of people who habitually live in the wild are much more acute than those of any one whose abode is within the pale of civilization. These jungle people live in a large degree by the use of their senses; those of the towns and cities by their wits."[60]

Robert Kohler's description of the "inner frontier" aptly characterizes the development patterns of southern Florida in the early decades of the twentieth century, where "wild and settled were unusually extensive and permeable."[61] Whereas southern Florida's commercial center had once been Key West, over a hundred miles south of the mainland, struggling settlements along the coastal ridge, such as Miami and Coconut Grove, were becoming increasingly important tourist destinations and cities in their own right. The creation of southern Florida's inner frontier, and related rapid transformations in the landscape's characteristics, corresponded to this era of fieldwork at Royal Palm, and as Kohler argued, facilitated the naturalists' work. For instance, the Old Ingraham Highway was completed in 1916, linking Miami to Royal Palm. It took several days for naturalists to reach the hammock during the first few years of survey work, but with the building of the Old Ingraham Highway, naturalists and others were able to reach Royal Palm in an afternoon.

As Karl Jacoby has shown, conservation projects have historically constructed local landscape practices as degrading to the environment. As an antidote and in opposition, conservationist discourses privilege techno-expertise as a more rational approach to managing land and resources.[62] The field history of Royal Palm suggests not only that conservationist projects called upon scientific knowledge to establish the site's worth for protection, but also that field scientists embodied a conservationist ethos. Naturalists' surveys and fieldwork were used both to justify efforts to protect the site from local usages and to construct locals as generalized threats to the hammock's ecological value.

Hunters' stories of Royal Palm circulated for years before surveying or fieldwork began at the site; even Florida's governors, at the far reaches of the state, were aware of the hammock's fame.[63] Yet it was the naturalists' reports of Royal Palm's tropical rarity that brought the hammock national attention and supported protectionist movements. Not inconsequential to the construction of the hammock's *natural* value was the generification of the site's human occupation and history. For these naturalists, all signs of "civilization," to use their racially charged term, signaled a generic threat to the hammock's integrity. Naturalists perceived the abundant evidence of the hammock's social life as an extension of the processes of land transformation occurring elsewhere. Seminole peoples, when mentioned at all, were treated as somehow naturalized to the site, but white gladesmen epitomized the possibilities of encroachment and, therefore, were seen as external to the hammock's history. By portraying the white glades community as out of place, naturalists' accounts smooth out the complex political economy and cultural significance of local landscape practices. It is as if the landscape's mysterious magic cast a shadow over the history of Indian removal, multicultural exchange networks, rural poverty, and related practices of production that mark Royal Palm as being both known and appreciated outside the confines of fieldwork.

CONCLUSION: PARADISE LOST

Ed Brewer named the island hammock he guided Hugh Willoughby to in 1897 "Paradise."[64] Years later, when Brewer's Paradise became the first protected area within the Everglades, it was rechristened Royal Palm State Park.[65] Charles Torrey Simpson advocated keeping the name "Paradise Key," noting that six other hammocks in the Everglades also offered substantial stands of royal palms, with a hammock on Cape Romano to the northwest containing five hundred of the trees.[66] Simpson was troubled with the appropriate "priority" of naming, as Cape Romano's hammock had been called Royal Palm for many years.[67] Although the concern was valid, the renaming of the hammock is indicative of the larger smoothing out process that occurs when landscapes become valued for their ecological rarities, even when these rarities, the royal palms, were not quite so rare.

Brewer's Edenic nomination ironically foreshadowed his eventual banishment from the hammock's genealogy of knowledge production and human history. Nowhere in the scholarly literature on the hammock is there mention of Ed Brewer. Brewer, like countless others who assisted naturalists and surveyors throughout the Everglades, had the specialized knowledge of the Everglades backcountry that made him the natural choice to act as guide and informant. Yet the landscape's natural history embodies a tension, which continues today, that posits a distinction between expert knowledge and local practices, blurring the correlation between these two knowledge regimes.

It is as if ecological fame making is a process that effaces all other landscape visions from our popular consciousness, turning the landscape into what Bruno Latour called a "smooth object." Smooth objects, Latour explained, are materialities containing clearly defined boundaries and essences, "matters of fact," belonging "without any possible question to the world of things, a world made up of persistent, stubborn, non-mental entities defined by strict laws of causality, efficacy, profitability, and truth."[68] Smoothing out is a process of disentangling. When places become ecologically famous, belonging solely to the world of things and facts, their social natures are polished smooth, removing discordances — in the case of Royal Palm, the history of access, use, racialization, and transformation of lands by peoples in conflict and accord.

To account for the incongruity of discovering an unknown landscape in the midst of a clearly lived-in place, naturalists practiced a form of selective recognition through rhetorical strategies. First, in constructing the site as worthy of their fieldwork, in other words as an isolated tropical Paradise, naturalists constructed certain people, the Seminoles, as naturalized to the landscape and treated other people, rural whites, both as out of place and as threats to the continued viability of the hammock's unique biota. Second, the literature repeatedly discounts the relationship between local landscape practices and place-based knowledge, constructing these forms of residential knowledge as being distinctly inferior to understandings gained through fieldwork.

My personal connection to the Everglades landscape and to the national park has granted me great sympathy to these early naturalists' concerns and sense of despair. But the costs of this generification have been high and were disproportionately meted out. Although locals continued to hunt in the park for several decades, their activities were treated as criminal, mirroring their prepark constructions, and hunters' lives were marked by a poetics of detection avoidance, underground economies, and disciplinary action. Traditional subsistence and commercial practices became "emparked," a mode of power that Joe Hermer has argued characterizes the legislatively defined stewardship of North American parks and protected areas.[69]

This generification was also instrumental to contemporary narratives of the landscape. The visitor's experience of Royal Palm is of a landscape curiously devoid of human history. The countless interpretive materials at the site make no mention of the various peoples who once considered the hammock home or depended upon it for their livelihoods. Other locations in the park do provide some historical interpretation, though in the form of the familiar stories of human-induced ecological disaster: plume hunters and the near extinction of glorious wading birds, drainage schemes and habitat loss, and the threat of introduced species to native biota.

The Story Doesn't End with the Ambush on the Sebastian River Bridge

> I wish I had told this story twenty-five or thirty years ago when these
> outlaws had relatives and friends living and people who had heard
> and doubted the way that they were captured. I regret that very much.
> —OREN B. PADGETT, *O. B. Padgett: The Native Son,*
> *the Lawman, the Prisoner, the Citizen*

On November 1, 1924, sheriff's deputies ambushed John Ashley and three other gang members as they tried to flee the state. The months prior to the gang's final flight had been marked by increased violence and decreased community support. Before they were captured, the men had intended to drive from southern Florida to Jacksonville, where they hoped to spend the night with one of Ashley's sisters, and then to continue on to California, where they would start new lives.

Things had begun to go badly earlier in the year. In February, a predawn raid surprised Ashley, who was staying at an island camp located about two miles from his parents' home. With John Ashley that night were Laura Upthegrove, his father Joe, and another man. They slept in three tents set up adjacent to a hundred-gallon copper still. The successful raid was the culmination of several frustrating months of searching by Sheriff Bob Baker's deputies. In fact, for days prior to the raid, deputies Fred Baker and H. L. Stubbs had searched the swamps on their hands and knees in order to avoid detection as they pinpointed the camp's exact location.

As the deputies crept up to the tents at three in the morning, Laura Upthegrove's mongrel dog, Old Bob, began to bark. A deputy shot the dog, and a "hail of bullets" followed, as John Ashley described the events to Hix C. Stuart. Joe Ashley (killed while putting on his boots) and Deputy Fred Baker died in the cross fire. Several rounds of buckshot pierced Laura Upthegrove's scalp and thighs. Her terrible screams, according to Sheriff Bob Baker, caused the deputies to stop shooting. John Ashley escaped unharmed into the woods.

When the deputies approached the camp, they discovered Laura Upthegrove and several women relatives who had heard the shots and come running. The deputies arrested all the women, including John's mother, two of his grown sisters, a sister-in-law, and a three-year-old child, and took them to jail. Later, John's brother Bill and his brother-in-law Wesley Mobley were arrested. All the family members were subsequently released, though Laura was held for nearly two months. While the family was in jail, a mob enraged over Fred Baker's death burned several Ashley family homes, including that of Ashley's now-widowed mother.

John Ashley seemed brazenly nonchalant on the day he attempted to flee the state — particularly for a man who was at the time the target of a nine-month-long intensive manhunt. That afternoon he was seen strolling the streets of Fort Pierce, having a shave and a haircut, and then playing a game of pool. As night fell, Ashley and his companions — Ray Lynn, Clarence Middleton, and Hanford Mobley, Ashley's nineteen-year-old nephew — climbed into Ashley's Ford touring car and headed northward on the Old Dixie Highway. Young Mobley was driving.

In all likelihood, Ashley's party was not surprised to find the Sebastian River bridge chained off, marked with a hanging red lantern. O. B. Padgett, a deputy at the scene, noted in his memoirs that it had been raining for the preceding few days and so the road was washed out in several places between Fort Pierce and the Sebastian River, a distance of twenty-eight miles. Just a few miles earlier that evening, the group had already driven through another short detour, similarly marked with red caution lights, lending further credibility to the roadblock they encountered at the Sebastian River bridge. On the other hand, Ashley may not have had a chance to think at all. Tipped off earlier in the day to the gang's flight, six deputies and the sheriff of Saint Lucie County lay hidden in the tall grass along the roadbed. As soon as Ashley's car slowed, the men leapt out and thrust their automatic rifles into the passengers' faces.

What happened next on that dark stretch of road has been the subject of heated speculation for the past eighty years. All accounts concur, however, that the deputies shot and killed Ashley, Mobley, Lynn, and Middleton not long after stopping their car. The deputies then tossed the bodies into the back of Ashley's Ford ("like a stack of cordwood," as the saying goes) and drove them back to Fort Pierce. There they laid the men out in the grass in front of Will Fee's Hardware Store and Mortuary in downtown Fort Pierce. A curious crowd soon gathered to stare at the dead outlaws. Immediately rumors emerged that the men had been killed while handcuffed ("in cold blood"). Two young men who happened across the bridge just after the Ashley Gang was captured testified that the men were handcuffed when they saw them; other witnesses claimed they saw handcuff marks on the bodies when they arrived in Fort Pierce. At the inquest the deputies told a different story. They testified that the men were reaching for their guns and resisting arrest when they were shot. The judge, after calling one mistrial, ruled the deaths justifiable homicide. Since then, two of the deputies have provided detailed accounts that suggest that the men actually were already handcuffed at the time of the shooting.

John Ashley, Hanford Mobley, and Ray Lynn (since no one claimed his body) were buried in the Ashley family cemetery the next day. They were buried next to John's three brothers and father, all of whom had previously been killed while participating in gang activities. Laura Upthegrove arranged for the Salvation Army to conduct the graveside service.

6. ALLIGATOR CONSERVATION, COMMODITIES, AND TACTICS OF SUBVERSION

It speaks to the sheer ingenuity of culture that the alligator, such an unlikely creature, has been called upon to meet so many different human needs. The reptiles may weigh hundreds of pounds, can grow to sixteen feet (though about thirteen feet is considered large today), and are certainly cumbersome to transport. Their bodies are elongated and lizard-like. The dermal layer of alligator skin consists of scales, called "scutes," with bony plates, called "buttons," embedded in the skin, all creating a tough armor. Alligator jaws are massively strong vices used to impale and crush prey. Alligators grasp larger prey in their jaws and roll in the water, drowning whatever it is, including on rare occasions people. Suffice it to say, hunting alligators can be both difficult and dangerous.

Still, ever since humans and alligators have coexisted, the reptiles' flesh and skin have been rendered into a dazzling array of products. For the most part these products have been commodities, or items produced for exchange in the capitalist marketplace. To a large degree, the hunter's landscape is an assemblage organized around the tasks of commodifying alligators. Recent scholarship into nature's commodification has highlighted the importance of paying attention to the material specificity of nature itself.[1] For instance, by the time alligators become belts, boots, or bags, they have become exchangeable equivalents (via the intermediary of money) to similar products produced from cow's leather. Money, as Noel Castree has noted, "can buy you anything from a carbon credit to a medicinal plant to an alligator."[2] Yet the commodification process involved in turning a living animal into monetized value, as Castree contends, differs substantially depending upon whether the production process begins in the cattle pastures of central Texas

Photograph originally captioned "William Holding Gator, Madeira Hammock, Florida." Photograph by Julian Dimock, February 1906; printed by permission of the American Museum of Natural History.

or the swamps of southern Florida. Although similar in the abstract, each process of commodification has its own logic that orders the socionatural relations of production. Alligators are undomesticated reptiles that live in underground caves, a material reality intrinsic to how they were hunted and prepared for the market.

These same material constraints and specificities posed a challenge to the state's attempts at intervening in the alligator-hide trade. Since the 1930s, alligator hunting has been banned or restricted in many parts of Florida. Various legal barriers to alligator hunting included restrictions on the size and sex of animals legally taken, the imposition of closed hunting seasons and countywide hunting bans, and the creation of protected areas. Hunters tended to ignore or resist these restrictions, making antihunting ordinances and related disciplinary procedures fairly ineffective in stemming the tide of alligator hunting in the Everglades. Simply put, glades families had very few economic alternatives to hunting and so went to great lengths to subvert the law's territorial claims. The hide market's global networks of production and distribution supported this oppositional politics.

Very few alligator lives were saved by the criminalization of alligator hunting. Instead, these restrictions fundamentally altered glades hunting by transforming customary economic practices into criminal behavior. As Karl Jacoby has shown, the history of U.S. conservation approaches has revolved around the "twin axes" of "law" and "lawlessness." Regulating and conserving wilderness and emplaced species required the institution of new crimes, notably the "transformation of previously acceptable practices into illegal acts: hunting or fishing redefined as poaching, foraging as trespassing, the setting of fires as arson, and the cutting of trees as timber theft."[3] Explicit in this conservationist approach is the construction of rural folk as reckless criminals incapable of managing local environments for the common good.

With the criminalization of alligator hunting, new tactics of subversion became entangled with the refrains of earth, fire, and flesh. Tactics of subversion, as I examine below, ranged from outright violent resistance to radically altered practices of mobility and territoriality. These changes occurred at multiple scales and for different strategic purposes. Yet taken together, they posed a significant challenge to the state's ability to maintain control over its territory and resources. Although alligator-conservation measures may not have had the practical outcome desired, the state's contradictory vision of nature (particularly alligator nature) is made visible through these laws and practices, as I show in this chapter.

ALLIGATOR AS COMMODITIES

Although meat and leather goods have been the most important products derived from the alligator, the reptile has been used for numerous esoteric purposes. During the Civil War, alligator fat was used to lubricate machinery for the cotton industry and also to make soap.[4] At the end of the nineteenth century, a lively market existed in alligator teeth, which were selling for four dollars per pound, which would equal the teeth from six alligators.[5] Tourist shops today continue to sell large alligator skulls and stuffed baby alligators, often mounted on Florida-shaped plaques. Until the late 1940s, live baby alligators were sold by the thousands to Florida visitors and shipped to northeastern pet shops. Few of these animals survived, and those that did were often released into nearby lakes and ponds, creating a nuisance and leading to a variety of urban legends about alligators inhabiting city sewer systems.

Throughout American history, Native peoples and settlers of the southeastern swamps have eaten alligator meat, which tastes a bit like fishy chicken. Most commonly, the edible portion—a long strip of meat, about two inches wide, from each side of the alligator's tail—was cut into chunks and pan fried. Today's farm-raised alligator meat is taken from other parts of the animal as well, its flavor "enhanced" by a variety of rubs and marinades, and served fried, stewed, or sautéed in butter and spices. Though alligator meat is growing in popularity, partly because it is considered fairly healthy, it was not a favorite with commercial alligator hunters. When I asked one hunter if he ever ate the alligator's meat after removing the hides, he said, "When you sees what you's squeezing out of them . . ." as his thoughts trailed off.

But fine leather goods made from the reptile's soft underbelly have been, and continue to be, the alligator's most marketable product. The high demand for alligator hides supported and shaped southern rural economies for almost a century, not only in Florida but also in the bayous of Louisiana, the swamps of southern Georgia, and the coastal Carolinas. Small, localized markets for alligator goods have existed for some time—for instance,

John James Audubon commented on the use of alligator skins for shoes, saddlebags, and boots in the late 1700s. The market for alligator leather increased substantially during the Civil War when a naval blockade of southern ports created a shortage of cowhide.[6] During this period, the increasing availability of reliable and powerful firearms, with greater muzzle velocity and bullets that could pierce the reptile's tough skin, revolutionized alligator hunting.[7] After the war, alligator leather remained in great demand for footwear, traveling bags, belts, card cases, and other items.[8] Estimates from the Florida Game and Fresh Water Fish Commission (FGFC) suggest that during a ten-year period, ending in 1891, Florida commercial hunters and sportsmen killed 2.5 million alligators,[9] though these estimates are difficult to verify. Certainly, tens of thousands of alligators were killed each year for the hide trade in the early period of Florida's statehood. Even so, demand for alligator leather far exceeded supply, and by 1900, importers were bringing in caiman skins from Central America and Mexico and selling them as American alligator.[10]

During this era of peak demand, Florida became the chief supplier of American alligator hides to East Coast tanneries. In 1902, tanneries in the United States produced approximately 280,000 skins annually, worth about $420,000 (more than $10 million in today's dollars), with about 22 percent of the alligator hides originating in Florida.[11] Nineteenth-century leather products followed the vagaries of fashion, though ladies' handbags, men's belts, and footwear always remained strong sellers. Matched panels from larger hides were transformed into high-quality luggage and handbags; smaller items, such as wallets, billfolds, shoes, and belts, were made from skin from the alligator's throat, neck, and flank as well as from scraps.[12]

Transforming live alligators into handbags utilized the labor of hide buyers, leather importers, exporters, designers, manufacturers, and advertisers. But the production process began in the field, where hunters killed and skinned the animals. Even in the field, the market governed the methods of hide preparation, a curious moment in which the "invisible hand" guided the actual cutting and gutting in the production process. Hide buyers, based on the dictates of the market, determined whether only the alligator's soft belly, referred to as a "flatskin," would be taken or whether the entire hide would be removed. When the entire hide was taken, a process called "horn-backing," the tougher back skin (or dorsal scales), head, and feet remained on the hide.[13] From the 1940s through the 1960s, alligator purses that featured an intact head, claws, and tail were the rage among tourists. Larger alligators were skinned flat, as were the smaller alligators unless the hunter knew in advance that a buyer required a specific number of hornbacked hides. Though preparing hornbacked hides required additional effort, hunters obliged, as their cash value was higher. Hunters were well aware of the market's role in the production process, and they sought out the larger, more valuable alligators and prepared the skins based on market desirability.

After the hides were preserved with salt, hunters sold them through a loose network of hide buyers. In some cases hide buyers traveled throughout the state, acting as brokers between hunting households and larger buyers. In other communities a local hunter acted as a buyer, making a small profit off each hide, before transporting the hides to the larger hide buyers. Hide buyers negotiated out of the backs of their trucks, from their back porches, and at isolated trading posts throughout the Everglades. Hide buyers then shipped accumulated hides to tanneries in Louisiana and New York.

Albert Reese cited a U.S. Bureau of Fisheries report that shows a gradual rise in price between 1891, when hide prices averaged sixty cents per skin, and 1902, when hides averaged ninety cents, with larger hides worth up to two dollars.[14] For the year 1898, Anthony Dimock reported that the prices alligator hunters received ranged from one dollar a hide for hides measuring seven feet or more to as little as ten cents a hide for those less than four feet long.[15] Table 1 gives the numbers of alligator hides bought by Florida hide buyers, the average prices paid for seven-foot hides, and these values adjusted for inflation into 2010 dollars. The demand for hides remained high from the late 1800s on, and the prices hunters received increased incrementally through the 1930s. During and after World War II, alligator hide values increased substantially.

By the 1930s, prices had risen to between twenty-five cents for a three-foot hide to three dollars for a seven-footer.[16] Given that an average Depression-era laborer's wage was two dollars per day, this was "good money." At these prices, those who hunted full-time could easily earn an adequate living.

Table 1. Estimated number and price of alligator hides sold in Florida per year

Year	Number of hides sold	Average price for seven-foot hides (dollars)	Adjusted average price for seven-foot hides (in 2010 dollars)
1929	190,000	1.50	19.01
1930	188,000	2.50	32.45
1931	150,000	2.75	39.21
1932	145,000	2.75	43.51
1933	130,000	2.75	45.85
1934	120,000	3.00	48.52
1935	162,000	3.00	47.46
1936	150,000	3.00	46.78
1937	130,000	4.00	60.21
1938	110,000	4.00	61.49
1939	80,000	5.25	81.86
1940	75,000	7.00	108.37
1941	60,000	8.75	129.01
1942	18,000	15.75	209.43
1943	6,800	19.25	241.17
1944	7,000	21.00	258.61
1945	12,000	22.75	273.94
1946	10,000	15.75	175.06
1947	25,000	13.30	129.27
1949	25,000	14.00	127.49

Sources: E. Ross Allen and Wilfred T. Neil, "Increasing Abundance of the Alligator in the Eastern Portion of Its Range," *Herpetologica* 5, no. 6 (1949): 109–12, except the figures for 1949, which are from Florida Game and Fresh Water Fish Commission, "Gator Conservation Committee Makes Management Suggestions," *Florida Wildlife* 3, no. 12 (1949): 22; the average price for seven-foot hides in 1949 is the average price for all sizes of hides sold.

Full-time alligator hunting was the exception, however, as most glades families depended on alligator hides for only a portion of their yearly income. Instead, alligator hunting represented one of an array of Everglades-based income activities that also included commercial and subsistence fishing and farming, frog and turtle hunting, and otter, mink, and raccoon trapping. Because farming, trapping, and fishing are seasonal income generators, hide income was a critical source of supplemental funds even for occasional hunters.

Alligators as commodities were central to the organizational logic of the hunter's landscape, with the market intervening to shape practices in the field (for instance, determining whether it was the alligator's hide, meat, teeth, or bones that were harvested and how these parts were prepared for sale). Next to the market, the law was the most notable intervention in the hunter's territorial claims and practices. For gladesmen the law represented a constellation of indictments, offenses, penalties, judicial procedures, and practices of enforcement. In interviews, hunters used the term "the law" to represent a complex political and economic system that recast their customary practices into a suite of illegal practices known as poaching. These antihunting regulations, as well as the related enforcement and disciplinary procedures, reflect the state's vision of alligators as nature *and* as objects of consumption.

The FGFC was the main arbitrator of the law, setting and enforcing alligator-hunting policy throughout the state. Although the agency has had several incarnations, this branch of the state government was first established in 1913 with the constitutional authority to set hunting and fishing regulations, levy fees for violations, hire county game wardens, and enact a system of hunting licenses.[17] In all, the FGFC retained extraordinary power over all of the state's terrestrial and freshwater aquatic life.[18]

The FGFC began producing biennial (and later annual) reports of its activities in 1914, and though they vary in format and content from issue to issue, these reports consistently outline the agency's law enforcement and natural resource conservation activities. During the first decades of the FGFC's wildlife oversight, alligators were simply not mentioned in the reports, either as a game resource or in terms of hunting licensing or violations. In fact, the FGFC does not mention alligators in its reports until 1936. Until that time, alligators as a category of state interest appear negligible. Instead, the agency's reports include extensive statistics on squirrels, turkeys, early or late season quail, deer, and other species, providing information by region on the economic values of each species and on the numbers of each taken by hunters.

Conservationist approaches, based on progressive politics, guided wild-life management during this period in American history. This approach, most famously advocated by President Theodore Roosevelt, sought to manage natural resources "scientifically" to ensure long-term sustainable harvests, both maximizing economic potential and preventing widespread environmental destruction.[19] Particularly in the FGFC's early years, when report after report contained charts detailing the economic value of Florida game, the agency's mission and evaluation of its practices reflected this conservationist game management approach. Conversely, the agency's lack of attention to alligator issues in the first twenty-two years of its history suggests that alligators apparently were considered neither an economic nor a natural resource requiring state oversight.

The invisibility of the alligator in the first decades of the FGFC's oversight is curious. Clearly the trade in alligator hides was economically significant. During this period, Florida was a top supplier of alligator hides to tanneries, and for the most part, prices steadily increased. Moreover, alligator hunting was ubiquitous in rural swamp communities throughout the state. Still, the FGFC did not consider the alligator a game species worthy of regulation. No doubt several reasons contributed to this absence, including the fact that alligators, in their amphibious saurian splendor, did not fit into the state's existing categories of game. Alligators are not freshwater fish (caught by line or net), they are not fur-bearing animals (trapped by various means), they are not land mammals (tracked and shot), and they are not ducks or other fowl (called and shot).

Most important, alligators inhabited landscapes considered detrimental to the state's developmental interests. Swamps were considered miasmic, dangerous, and certainly unproductive, and reclamation remained official federal and state policy well into the twentieth century. Within this political and economic context, there was no reason for the state to take an interest in the population dynamics of alligators. The period between 1906 and 1928 is really the early period of swampland drainage in the Everglades, as Robert Walker and William Solecki demonstrate in their examination of changes in land cover and in land use in the Everglades.[20] During this period, state policy was directed at promoting drainage for agricultural development, and lands were transferred to both industrial concerns and small farmers for this purpose. By the economic crises of the 1930s, the major features of the current drainage system were already in place, though farmers often faced flooding and uncertain conditions.[21]

Along the same lines, the rural poor who depended on these swamps for their livelihoods were equally absent from the developmental interests of the state. Florida at the turn of the last century was dreaming of empire. Commercial alligator hunting evokes few of the gentlemanly images associated with Gilded Age sportsmen. Certainly, managing alligators to protect them as an economic resource for the rural poor was not a priority for the state.

That situation changed in the late 1930s, though not because the state began to view the species as a game resource. Instead, the state's economic imperatives began to change as the tourist industry altered in the 1930s. Whereas Miami, Palm Beach, and other popular resort areas had primarily been destinations for the wealthy in early decades, the 1930s brought an increasing number of middle-class vacationers to Florida. By the late 1930s, Florida was ready to reclaim its image as a major tourist destination. In 1939, the year the FGFC first called for a closed hunting season, the Federal Writers' Project (of the Work Projects Administration) published its *Florida: A Guide to the Southernmost State*.[22] As David Kadlec asserts, the Florida guide reads like an extended promotional brochure in which Florida's history, industry, and the arts all "revolve around tourism."[23] Certainly the state's natural landscapes, or at least a simulacrum of nature produced for visitors, was critical to the political economy of Florida tourism. In 1940 an estimated 2 million visitors came to Miami, making it the most popular destination in Florida.[24] These middle-class tourists often drove southward through the Everglades, stopping along the way at Florida's famous roadside attractions, where alligators were star features.

The importance of alligators to the emerging tourist economy is reflected in state wildlife management directives. Alligators are first mentioned in FGFC reports in 1937, when the hide trade is described as "negligible" though "once a big item." At this time, the agency noted that "public opinion" was calling for a closed season on alligator hunting, reflecting a desire to protect an important symbol of the state's tourist economy.[25] Public opinion must have held considerable sway; two years later, in a reversal of the agency's prior analyses, the agency described the alligator hide trade as "extensive" and recommended a closed season.[26] In 1941 the alligator completely emerged from the brackish waters of official disregard to become "representative of Florida's distinctive wildlife." Importantly, this representation asserted itself even "in the minds of many who have never been to this State."[27] The focus of these early conservation efforts was on protecting the alligator's symbolic value within a burgeoning tourist economy rather than on safeguarding its value as a commodity within the hide industry or, for that matter, protecting alligators for their own sake. Instead, the animal was managed as a central and iconic feature of a nature produced and staged for visitors to southern Florida. Thousands of postcards, souvenir placemats, billboards, saltshakers, and other tchotchkes attest to the alligator's central role in Florida's tourist economy.

In response to alligator-conservation concerns, the Florida legislature began passing laws to restrict alligator hunting. Beginning in 1939, state laws were passed that specifically limited alligator hunting in a number of Florida counties, particularly counties within the Everglades. These statewide acts imposed sanctions and limitations (on alligator and crocodile hunting, the transportation of hides, or the selling of live alligators and crocodiles and their eggs) based on each county's population size. For instance, hunting seasons, rather than outright bans, were established for smaller counties. Yet separate legislation of 1939 completely outlawed the capture, injury, or killing of alligators and crocodiles within Dade County at the southern end of the Everglades.[28] Conviction under this law imposed stiff penalties, with fines ranging from one hundred to five hundred dollars and with the possibility of imprisonment for up to six months in the county jail.

It is difficult to evaluate how effective these laws were. First, criminalizing alligator hunting meant that available data about numbers of hides sold and prices per hide — such as those in Table 1 — are necessarily rough estimates of an underground economy. Second, although fewer alligator hides were sold in the 1940s than in the previous decades, the market demand for alligator leather kept prices high. For instance, the demand for alligator leather rose substantially during World War II, while military enlistments meant there were far fewer hunters, accounting for the dramatic rise in hide values during 1942, 1943, 1944, and 1945. To put it in context: in 1944, the value of a seven-foot hide was twenty-one dollars and the federal minimum wage rate was thirty cents per hour. The value of alligator hides decreased

Vintage postcard. Note the caption: "All the Way from Florida."

after the war, though it remained relatively high. In 1949, for instance, President Harry S. Truman increased the minimum wage to seventy-five cents per hour. That same year, hides of all sizes were selling for about fourteen dollars each. Therefore, a hunter on a two-week trip could expect to bring back at least fifty hides and earn an income equivalent to several months' pay at a low-wage job.

But the postwar years were also a time of unprecedented landscape transformation in the Everglades. In 1947, Everglades National Park was established, and 1.3 million acres of land became off-limits to legal hunting (though as I discuss below, this was not a real deterrent to hunters). More importantly, the implementation of the massive Central and Southern Florida Project in 1948 supported the transition of wetlands to other land uses or other cover types on a massive scale.[29] The establishment of water-conservation areas and the Everglades Agricultural Area, as well as the C & SF Project's

Vintage postcard advertising an alligator farm tourist attraction. The back of the card reads "Alligators are extremely rare in Florida, having been hunted for their skin until practically extinct."

thousands of miles of canals and associated levees, dikes, and other water management devices, facilitated the expansion of agriculture and population growth in the Everglades. Earlier drainage efforts had offered the dream of an agricultural empire; the C & SF Project provided flood control security that allowed southern Florida agriculture to reliably serve national markets. From 1950 to 1970, at the height of the C & SF Project implementation, southern Florida's population tripled to nearly 2.5 million persons. These processes of change, which led to the transformation of half the historic Everglades, certainly had an impact on alligator habitats and alligator population dynamics. Even with relatively high prices for hides, the volume of hides sold in Florida never came near the numbers of the prewar years, because there were far fewer alligators to supply to the market.

SUBVERSIVE LANDSCAPES

If we understand alligator-protection laws as a manifestation of the state's vision of alligator nature, then that vision was literally embodied by FGFC wildlife officers, commonly called game wardens. Game wardens brought the state's constitutional authority over nature into the field and made the abstraction of government and law immediate and legible. Arguably, game wardens, underpaid civil servants for most of the agency's history, were the only points of contact between the larger political economy of wildlife management in Florida and local hunting practices. For glades hunters, game wardens were the law, a perspective seemingly shared by the wardens as well. James Huffstodt, a public information officer with the FGFC, has captured the essence of this embodiment: "The game warden is law in the Everglades. He is a cop, but a special cop whose sworn duty is to protect the state's wildlife resources from exploiters and poachers."[30] As Huffstodt's description suggests, game wardens mediated between the state's vision of nature and local practices of production. During this mediation, Everglades hunters were transformed into poachers.

Though antihunting legislation increased in severity from the late 1930s through the 1970s, little evidence suggests that game wardens had much success at actually apprehending hunters who were breaking the law. In the rare cases when hunters were arrested, typical sentences levied upon conviction were either a hundred-dollar fine or ninety days in jail. These fines were comparatively high, for other hunting violations, such as hunting deer out of season or shooting from highways, drew average fines of about ten to twenty dollars. Yet from 1939, when statewide restrictions were enacted, until 1966, only twenty-eight violations of alligator-hunting regulations are cited in the FGFC annual reports. These violations included the possession of alligator hides in a closed county, taking alligators in a closed season, and selling undersized hides.[31] Other listed violations may have applied to alligator hunters (hunting without a license, hunting at night with a light, and so on). Yet it is telling that only a few hunters were specifically cited for violations of laws applying to illegal alligator hunting, whereas endless pages of text catalog in minute detail citations for crimes against other species (the removal of a deer's sex organs, in one jarring example).

Even though the law may not have halted the hide trade (alligator purses were still flying off the shelf after thirty years of legislation), the law's politics did transform the culture and territorial practices of alligator hunting. In essence, the law transformed hunters into poachers, and this transformation in identity shaped the way hunters understood themselves in relation to the larger community and shaped their engagement with the landscape. The laws that outlawed and regulated alligator hunting radically altered the hunter's landscape, realigning the relations of humans and nonhumans in the process. Ultimately this realignment created a new landscape that I refer to as the "subversive landscape."

In the subversive landscape the law was always present, a danger constantly to be avoided. Gladesmen's stories portray a landscape where the law lurked behind every hammock or waited just beyond the horizon. In this new land, practices of invisibility, secrecy, and violence predominated. True, arrests were rare. But alligator hunters acted as if they were the persistent targets of the law's apparatus of surveillance and discipline. This abiding concern over the law's reach led alligator hunters to devise multiple strategies to subvert both the intention of antihunting legislation and game wardens' enforcement of these ordinances. These tactics of subversion included outright violence, covert acts of evasion, and, most significantly, the development of new territorial practices.

For the most part, hunters' resistance to the law involved solitary practices of evasion. Yet in rare instances, resistance included violent conflict. Reading between the lines in *Florida Wildlife*, the FGFC's magazine, we find a bleak history of harassment—shots fired into game wardens' cars and homes and even officers killed while attempting arrests. According to James Huffstodt's history of Everglades game wardens, twelve game wardens in the Everglades region died while on duty from 1946 to 1987, many while pursuing illegal hunters.[32] The book reads like an uninterrupted narrative of drawn pistols, smacks to the head, muttered curses, and shot-out tires, gas tanks, and windows.

After hunting became poaching, silence became part of the vernacular. Rural southerners tend to be fairly circumspect about their business affairs in general, and commercial hunters and fishermen have always avoided disclosing the locations of game and fish to avoid competition. Yet after alligator hunting became criminalized, hunters, with few exceptions, told no one outside their immediate families and close friends what they were doing. When former alligator hunters talk about their experiences, a constant refrain is the urgent need to "keep what you was doing to yourself." Poaching alligators became an exceedingly secret practice, in stark contrast to the openness that had characterized the first fifty years of the trade.

This secrecy entailed various strategies of staying hidden or being invisible within the landscape. When in the backcountry, hunters went to great lengths to hide their location. Spouses and children dropped hunters off, in the middle of the night, along remote country roads. From there, hunters would push their skiffs off into glades or, in the dry season, simply walk for miles through prairies to reach backcountry ponds. In case their jumping off spot had been disclosed or detected, hunters made sure they were picked up miles away at a different location. People literally covered their traces as they went, piling bunches of debris over ruts left by their boat hulls, dragging branches behind them as the walked to cover their footprints, and leaving conflicting and multiple tracks through the muck if using airboats or swamp buggies. Some hunters began working only at night, skinning their hides at dawn and then sleeping hidden within the deep recesses of hammocks or under their boats, which they camouflaged with vegetation.

Hunters developed habits of invisibility practiced across a million acres of difficult terrain, making the enforcement of hunting laws a staggering task. The landscape colluded in these evasions by providing refuge and revealing dangers. Until the 1950s, only a handful of game wardens patrolled the entire Everglades region, a span of 8 million acres. The utter flatness of the prairies made sneaking up on hunters almost impossible. An approaching vehicle or boat could be seen for miles. Covert action was equally unlikely in the mangrove jungles, as progress through that environment required portaging and chopping through the underbrush. Yet even with a significant increase in manpower and funding, curtailing alligator hunting in the Everglades would have been difficult. The story of one of the FGFC's most celebrated arrests illustrates the bureaucratic futility of stopping hunting in the Everglades. Breaking up "one of the most active alligator poaching rings in the history of the area" required four days, six law enforcement officers, three planes, and two swamp buggies.[33] The upshot of this massive effort? Three hunters were arrested at their backcountry camp and seventy hides were confiscated.

Game wardens may have been the embodiment of law and the state, but many were also locals who had grown up in communities in the very areas they patrolled. They shared common histories and friendships with the hunters and knew the hunters' families, and many wardens had once hunted and fished the Everglades marshes with the people they were now authorized to arrest.[34] In those cases, local connections created a great deal of ambiguity in the wardens' role as enforcers of game laws. Certainly, their personal experiences provided them insights into hunters' multiple strategies of resistance, as well as an intimate knowledge of the landscape. Compounding these ambiguities, community support for antihunting legislation and related disciplinary procedures was minimal. Word of mouth spread quickly when a game warden came around, allowing hunters to quickly conceal any hides left hidden around the house or barn. Even local magistrates and judges tended to turn a blind eye to illegal hunting, imposing only minimal fines (which could be recovered in a few nights' work), or were themselves hunters.[35]

Alligators contributed mightily to the evasive strategies of hunters. As Philippe Le Billon makes clear in his discussion of the geopolitics of resource wars, the state's ability to intercede in the appropriation of resources differs considerably depending upon the portability and spatial distribution of the resource under question. As Le Billon notes, oil and diamonds have material and discursive qualities very different from those of alligators and therefore "entail distinct social practices, stakes, and potential conflicts associated with their territorial control, exploitation, commercialization, and consumption."[36] The value of the alligator lay almost solely in its skin. Live alligators are large, unwieldy, and even dangerous, but alligator skins are highly portable and easy to conceal. Alligator hides could be stashed almost anywhere, sunk underwater, or buried in the muck. This commodity's intrinsic characteristics (pliable, lightweight, thin, immune to the elements) granted hunters a real material advantage over game wardens.

When out in the glades, unless absolutely necessary, hunters never kept their hides with them. Instead, they stashed them—rolled up and hidden on hammocks far from their camps or in a variety of containers such as old oil drums or "abandoned" coolers deep within saw grass thickets. As one man explained in an interview:

Wasn't no need to worry about the game warden or nothing like that.... If you was moving camp ... salt them over yonder in a cypress head until you started in, or something like that.

Alternatively, after removing the hides, hunters sank the carcasses in deep water or covered them with vegetation, also far from camp; otherwise the telltale sign of circling vultures would alert wardens and other hunters of their location from miles away. Since hunters avoided backtracking, they developed circuitous routes home, allowing them to hunt new marshes and ponds and still retrieve their hides without retracing their steps. For the most part, even when wardens approached hunters, they never found hides. People concealed their hides against their bodies under their clothes and tucked them into wading boots. Since game violators had to be caught with an alligator skin in his or her possession, hunters simply tossed their hides and guns into the water when a game warden appeared. One trick was to float a bag of trash in the water, marking where the hides had been sunk, then return later to retrieve the hides. Hunters never carried their hides to the road; instead, they kept them hidden in a nearby hammock or clump of higher ground until they were sure the coast was clear. Once at the road, hunters used modified vehicles to keep their hides hidden in secret boxes built into the beds of their trucks or in containers tucked inside engine compartments.

Yet, most significantly, the criminalization of alligator hunting altered the ways hunters asserted their customary rights to hunting territories. This shift in territorial practices occurred at multiple geographic scales and for different reasons. Prior to the criminalization of alligator hunting, customary hunting rights were based on a person's historic association with a particular region of the Everglades. By custom, gladesmen hunted within the region of the Everglades where they and their extended families lived. For instance, "west coast" hunters, those who lived in the communities around Everglades City and Chokoloskee, pursued game within the Ten Thousand Islands; the "Homestead boys" hunted the swamps in the southern Everglades.

Specific camps within these regions further solidified hunters' residential claims, and it would be hard to exaggerate the importance of the camps to this community's sense of place. As glades hunters moved through the landscape, tracking alligators and other game, they camped on any available high ground they could find. Although many camping spots were chosen out of necessity, glades hunters claimed certain places within the landscape as more permanent camping spots, what we might consider base camps. At some base camps, glades hunters kept canned goods (such as meat cooked down and preserved in lard), dry wood, or a change of clothes. These supplies were often left buried, hidden but ready for their return. Upon arriving at camp, they would shake out some dried grass and pile it up to form a higher place to lay their gear. At camp, hunters slept under a tarpaulin, tied taut with rope to trees and suspended about three feet above the ground. Hunters fashioned "skeeters bars" from cheesecloth or flour sacks that hung down from the tarpaulin and formed a loose curtain around the sleepers. They used whatever was handy — their rifles, axes, or blankets — to hold the skeeter bar down while they slept. At camp, hunters prepared hides, cleaned guns, sharpened knives and axes, slept, and lit fires to ward off the nighttime mosquitoes. Around these campfires they shared a drink, rolled and smoked cigarettes, and prepared dinner over an open fire.

Little differentiated these camps from the rest of the Everglades back-country, as few camps had permanent structures on them. Instead, only shared knowledge of others' territorial claims on the landscape distinguished one particular hammock or riverbank from another. Yet clearly these territorial claims were recognized as landscape practices that bound some people together and kept others apart, as Whidden's description of his Turnback Camp in the Corkscrew swamp suggests:

OGDEN: So you'd keep the same camp for the whole season?

WHIDDEN: Oh yeah. Year after year. Turnback Camp. . . . And the Browns, Jake Brown, and them from Immokalee, they camped down there too, but they camped maybe a half mile . . . down the road.

OGDEN: Did people share their camps, or did they have their own camps, usually?

WHIDDEN: No. Most people had their own camps, mostly. Well, you know, like, two of my uncles down there, they'd have a camp all to-gether there. . . . Maybe Sam would go into the woods with somebody, you know, somebody that wasn't even kin to him, or something like that. Maybe Bobby be in the woods with Stanley, you know. It just depends on who you wanted to go hunting with.

Whidden went on to explain that Turnback Camp was named for a turn in the road, a convenient spot for keeping the car hidden from game wardens. Thousands of these camps form invisible indices of a community's history within the landscape.

People who traditionally worked a certain area, say the mangrove swamps of the Bill Ashley Jungles, experienced the landscape as a network of trails and camps that spoke to a communal memory — such as stories of the Ashley Gang — while at the same time places within the landscape were claimed by particular hunters. Certain hunters allowed others to use their camps, if they were unoccupied, but other hunters had reputations that discouraged the use of their camps. Seldom did hunters meet each other in the Everglades backcountry — the landscape was simply too vast — and so conflicts related to hunting territories rarely arose. Some hunters did have reputations for violence, and so others understood those areas (and the animals therein) as completely off limits.

These customary claims to the landscape changed when hunters became poachers. Avoiding the law required being constantly on the move, shifting the locations of camps and even encroaching on others' hunting territories. Instead of staying within traditional territories, hunters shifted the location of where they worked, often based on gossip about the activities of local game wardens. So if things were getting "too hot" in one part of the Everglades, commercial hunters would pack up all their belongings (household, family, pets) and move to another region entirely. Previously, hunters had little incentive to move to other areas. When hunting in these new areas, gladesmen had little sense of the territory's localized jurisdictions (which camp belonged to which person) or of the obligations linked to these camps. These incursions created increasing animosity among hunters and a sense that outsiders were invading their territories. Thirty years later, former hunters talk disparagingly about the disrespectful practices of "west coasters," for instance.

The sense that one's territory was being encroached upon by outsiders suggests that customary understandings of the landscape remained in place. The Everglades continued to be experienced as an arena defined by individuals' claims and the community's response to those claims, as well as by larger histories and myths of place. Yet hunters also began to recognize and strategically manipulate other jurisdictional boundaries in their efforts to subvert the law. Until Florida passed a statewide ban on alligator hunting in 1962, counties defined hunting bans, specified closed seasons, and set other rules. So, for instance, in the southern Everglades, alligator hunting was completely banned in Dade County fairly early on yet remained legal in adjacent Monroe County for more than another decade.

Customary hunting territories did not overlap with country jurisdictions. Navigating the Everglades backcountry without maps, hunters had little sense of where one county ended and another began. Yet with the advent of county restrictions, hunters incorporated these new jurisdictional rules into their landscape practices. Some hunters moved throughout the landscape based on different regulations, for instance, moving into another county to hunt during open seasons. Most, however, strategically manipulated the ambiguity of the landscape for their own benefit. For example, the lines between Dade and Monroe counties would have been difficult for hunters or game wardens to determine, so hunters began to prefer areas that reflected this ambiguity. If stopped by game wardens, hunters could "play dumb," as one man described it, and because of the uncertainty of county boundaries, game wardens often let these hunters go. Most important, hunters made a practice of making sure that any hides they sold to buyers appeared to come from legal counties. Even if they had been hunting throughout Dade County, for instance, hunters came out of the "woods" in adjacent Monroe County. Others would hunt alligators at night from canals along deserted roads, throw the hides in the trunk of their cars, then drive across county lines.

James Scott has offered important insights into the politics and practices of resistance.[37] Following Scott, we might understand the glades hunters' subversive repertoire as practices of resistance that produce an indirect challenge to the state's authority. As Roderick Neumann has noted, the challenge these resistance strategies actually pose to the status quo has been debated, a discussion often revolving around differing interpretations of Antonio Gramsci's formulation of hegemony.[38] Neumann, in his analysis of poaching by Meru peasants in Tanzania's Arusha National Park, made the important point that although these acts, from illegal gathering of firewood to forest encroachment, may have multiple meanings and intentions, they are "political insofar as they represent a rejection of the state's claims of ownership and management."[39] Central to our understanding of hegemonic control is the recognition that the apparatus of power is dynamic and able to incorporate challenges to dominance either by accommodating or by dismantling these challenges.[40]

Certainly glades hunters' strategies of subversion effectively challenged the state's ability to govern. Subverting the state's claims to alligators involved the collaboration of humans and nonhumans: from the resistance strategies of hunters and communities to the material barriers intrinsic to the landscape and the commodified alligator. Hunting restrictions and bans altered the mobility of hunters (how, when, and where they moved through the Everglades). In turn, these subversion strategies (practiced across millions of acres of swamps and prairies) fundamentally altered glades hunters' experience of the landscape. As hunters became poachers, the Everglades became a different place, transformed from a landscape of customary practice to one of subversion. This landscape of subversion did not efface other meanings

and experiences of the Everglades, yet it entailed a crucial difference in hunters' practices of place, transforming the relations of humans and nonhumans in the process.

MARKET INTERVENTIONS

By the end of the 1940s, conservationists and the FGFC recognized that enforcement and disciplinary strategies were not working. The ability of FGFC
wildlife officers to prevent alligator hunting in the Everglades was nominal,
though the specter of the law certainly altered hunting practices and hunters' sense of place. Both the price of hides and the number of hides sold remained fairly constant in the late 1940s and early 1950s, even though there
was much less alligator habitat. After the war, these prices encouraged new
people into the hide market and may have intensified the hunting strategies
of long-term hunters.[41] Certainly the additional income allowed hunters to
purchase all-terrain vehicles, airboats, and even planes, which made their
apprehension even more difficult.

In response, in 1947 the Florida legislature enacted statewide bans on
hunting alligators during their spring mating season.[42] Two years later, in
the winter of 1949, the FGFC imposed a yearlong statewide moratorium on
alligator hunting, granting the agency time to determine appropriate management regulations. Members of the FGFC's alligator-conservation committee — which included biologists, commercial hide dealers, alligator farmers,
and sportsmen — agreed that in the Everglades region in particular, hunting was threatening alligators with extinction.[43] Hunters I have spoken with
seem to concur that during this period alligators were being overhunted in
the easily accessible waterways, such as canals or lakes near roads or marshes
that were within a few hours of a boat landing. "Weekend hunters" using
airboats and other new technologies were able to reach particular lakes and
wipe out all the alligators in one day, forcing more-traditional hunters using
poled skiffs to travel to ever-more-remote areas. Stories abound of hunters
working their way to a favorite hunting area, hacking through overgrown
mangroves, only to encounter piles of alligator carcasses along the bank,
vultures soaring in circles above. Though the state of Florida closed all legal
alligator hunting seasons in early 1962, an estimated $500,000 worth of hides

were sold that year in Miami alone.[44] In 1969, an investigation conducted by the *Miami Herald* estimated that 250 full-time hunters worked out of Everglades National Park and adjacent marshes and that over 2,000 other hunters worked in the same region on a part-time basis.[45]

With enforcement not working, the state shifted its approach. Instead of pursuing illegal hunting, the FGFC and other resource agencies went after the hide market. Several states, including New York, passed laws banning the sale of products from endangered species in 1969, the same year alligators were listed as endangered. Also that year, the Lacey Act of 1900 was amended to prohibit the interstate trade of animals taken illegally from their point of origin. Most alligator hunters acknowledge that these acts marked the end of alligator hunting in Florida. As Leonard Chesser described it, "Even to 1969 I never worked for no one in the summer. I was always 'gator huntin'"; for Chesser and others the Lacey Act changed this lifestyle for good.[46] In 1973, the landmark Endangered Species Act was passed, and under its auspices, the FGFC formally determined that alligators were under immediate threat of extinction. In total, these federal prohibitions completely shut down all the loopholes that sustained the illegal alligator-hide market.

With the end of the alligator-hide trade, alligator populations quickly increased to such a degree that in 1977 the alligator was reclassified as threatened.[47] By all accounts, the alligator has made a spectacular comeback, yet the extent of the comeback is nearly impossible to quantify. Although alligator hunting seems to have posed a serious threat to alligator populations in Florida, few scientific studies support this assertion.[48] However, the anecdotal evidence that hunting threatened the viability of alligators in the Everglades is hard to dismiss. For instance, in an interview published in *National Geographic* magazine in 1948, R. B. Storter recalled taking 10,000 alligator hides to Tampa during three months in 1898. Of these hides, 1,000 of the skins came from Roberts Lake, which Storter described as "one of the most fabulous gator 'mines' in the country."[49] The scientific community generally agreed that alligator populations were declining, particularly between 1950 and 1970, though this assessment was based on "subjective observations."[50] The FGFC only began conducting systematic surveys of Florida alligator populations after 1974. The results suggest that after federal protection and the shutdown of the hide markets, alligator populations increased dramatically. From 1974 to 1992, alligator densities on wetlands increased an average 41 percent.[51]

Alligators became so abundant after hunting stopped that instead of protecting alligators from humans, wildlife officers began spending their days protecting humans from alligators. In 1976, the FGFC received "between 8,000 to 10,000" alligator-related complaints, apparently too many to calculate accurately.[52] By the early 1980s, thousands of alligators per year were being harvested through the state's nuisance alligator management program. Under it, hunters receive 70 percent of the hide's value and permission to sell the meat while the state retains 30 percent of hide profits.[53] Other elements of the alligator management plan, developed through the years, include a lottery system for annual legal hunts, alligator farming and ranching programs, and the leasing of private wetlands for alligator hunting.[54] At this time, the state of Florida is in the midst of developing a new alligator management plan, one that will probably include open seasons on alligator hunting again.

CONCLUSION: POACHING, RESISTANCE, AND SUBVERSIVE LANDSCAPES

Though the methods for conserving alligators shifted over time, consistent to the rationale was an understanding of alligators as a form of common property. Alligator poaching thus became a form of trespass against this common property. In their analyses of English antihunting legislation during the eighteenth century, E. P. Thompson and Douglas Hay demonstrated the ways in which these acts extended class privilege, particularly rights over property as inclusive of rights to game.[55] The era's increasingly harsh penalties, including death, negated customary rights that had asserted a distinction between rights to land and the ownership of the animals that roamed the land. In doing so, these ordinances served to redistribute rights over animals along class lines. As Hay remarked, "True equality before the law in a society of greatly unequal men is impossible: a truth which is kept decently buried beneath a monument of legislation, judicial ingenuity and cant. But when they wrote the laws protecting wild game, the rulers of eighteenth-century England dispensed with such hypocrisies."[56]

Thankfully, the Everglades never served as the backdrop for *unmitigated* class warfare like that waged within the forests and parks of eighteenth-century England, though the violence and violent displacements were palpable. Yet Florida's antihunting legislation similarly entailed the redefinition of animals, in this case alligators, as a particular species of property and involved the redistribution of these animals along class lines. Although rural hunters in the Everglades always considered alligators a form of common property, with the allocation of this property being determined through informal rules linked to territory, antihunting legislation established the animals as another form of common property — albeit one that excluded hunters. Instead, the "common" of this public good was intrinsic to ideas about the Everglades as a particular form of landscape. In the early years of alligator conservation, the reptiles were considered crucial to the visitors' experiences and expectations of this great and "exotic" swamp.

Less visibly, the reconfiguration of the commercial hide trade as poaching marked a larger shift in the political ecology of the Everglades. Hunting in the Everglades was hardly the largest threat to alligator viability. When Daniel Beard, Everglades National Park's first superintendent, surveyed the natural resources of the proposed park in 1938, he concluded that hunting posed a serious threat to alligator populations within the southern Everglades.[57] Aside from Seminole hunters, Beard estimated that twenty to thirty white men were regularly hunting within the proposed park boundaries. But with great insight, Beard linked drainage-induced changes in Everglades hydrology to alligator vulnerability. Beard's visit corresponded with an exceptionally dry winter, which would have made the alligators congregating in available lakes and sloughs even in the predrainage Everglades more accessible to area hunters. Yet Beard suggested that drainage operations compounded this seasonal dryness, leaving the Everglades unnaturally dry and thus increasing the alligators' vulnerability to hunters.[58]

Drainage not only made alligators more vulnerable to hunters, it also greatly reduced their habitat range and population viability. As early as 1915, the zoologist Albert Reese argued that although hunting and "wanton sport" was of concern, drainage efforts represented the most serious threat to the alligator population in Florida.[59] Drainage altered alligator habitat not only by lowering water levels but also, more obviously, by transforming the Ever-glades into developable land. As the dredging equipment ground deter-minedly through miles of interior wetlands, early naturalists began warning of the ecological consequences of drainage and changes in land use. Charles Torrey Simpson eloquently described this transformation: "The Everglades which teemed with life and were clothed with splendid vegetation are fast becoming a flat, uninteresting farm country."[60] The metamorphosis of the Everglades from what historian David McCally calls a "derelict system" to a "developmental" landscape occurred rapidly, particularly picking up mo-mentum after 1948.[61] By the time the Lacey Act was amended, half the his-toric Everglades had been drained, with approximately 30 percent of the historic landscape converted to agricultural and urban land uses. The brunt of the urban development occurred along the southeastern coast, causing the destruction of peripheral marshes where alligators were once abundant.[62] The concurrent human pressures of market-driven hunting, changing water levels and cycles, and extensive habitat loss intersected at the same time across the same landscape to threaten alligator populations in the Everglades. Ask-ing which of these factors was most critical to the viability of Everglades alli-gator populations poses an unanswerable question. Even determining what predrainage alligator populations were is a task that F. J. Mazzotti and L. A. Brandt described as "impossible."[63]

EPILOGUE: THE BILL ASHLEY JUNGLES
Trace Impressions of a Forgotten Landscape

In this book I have used the term "territorial assemblage" to describe those collectives of humans and nonhumans engaged in tasks that result in the demarcation of territory. Landscapes are the product of these assemblages. The territorial claims upon these landscapes extend far beyond the boundaries of southern Florida. No book could do justice to this rhizomic proliferation. My own interests have led me to focus on the territorial assemblages that intervene in the lives of glades hunters. Their experience of the landscape is the lens through which I consider the presence and politics of alligators, mangroves, water, fire, mythic snakes, and the like.

Almost every aspect of the Ashley Gang—real and imagined—is compelled by nature's politics. Certainly the gang's notoriety stems, in part, from its close association with a landscape considered dangerous, inscrutable, and worthless. Like creatures from the Saturday afternoon matinees of my childhood, the Ashleys appeared to be *of the swamp*. The politics of this swampiness is straightforward. Only people who made their living from the Everglades (in other words, rural and poor people) would have been able to form this close association in the first place. At the same time, their intimacy with the landscape provided them with the means to subvert the law for many years.

As if unbidden, trace impressions of the Ashley Gang continue to appear on the Everglades landscape. These appearances have the power to reconfigure all kinds of territorial claims in the process. For instance, archaeologists excavating mounds in Boynton Beach, Florida, were upset to find that looters searching for Ashley Gang treasure had already disturbed the sites.[1] Similar inclinations toward plunder led folks to loot the Ashley family cemetery in

The Bill Ashley Jungles.
Photograph by Keith Bradley.

the 1960s.[2] Today, the cemetery has been restored, though it no longer lies in the swampy periphery of Palm Beach County. Instead, the upscale Mariner Sands gated community—which features championship golf courses, a croquet greensward, and a doggie park—now maintains the grounds below which John Ashley rests. In this manicured cemetery social stratification is manifest.

We find further traces of the Ashley Gang in the Bill Ashley Jungles, a large expanse of coastal mangrove swamp and hammock islands formed by the headwaters of the East River in Everglades National Park, well over a hundred miles from the Ashley Gang cemetery. Glen Simmons, like many old-time alligator hunters, loved the Bill Ashley Jungles for its plentiful game and isolation. This is an exceedingly remote part of the southern Everglades that few outsiders visited until the mid-twentieth century. Describing the region's confusing scatter of mangrove islands and meandering creeks, Simmons once said that from above the Bill Ashley Jungles would look like the tangled roots of a very large old tree. From above, it does appear entangled. But such a perspective—for example, the one provided by an aerial photograph or a national park map—reveals only some of the landscape's entanglements. Certainly such a perspective will suggest the difficulties of navigation in the mangrove jungles. Yet more than these biotic mangles confound the easy arborescence of tree logic.

At the turn of the last century, John Ashley and his brother Bill capitalized on this isolation by staying hidden in these southern swamps for several months. While there, the brothers hunted alligators and otters together and lived off wild birds and the occasional deer. In the years after John died, Bill spent many more months in these remote jungles trying to distance himself literally and metaphorically from his brother's notorious crimes. Bill was the oldest son in the Ashley family. He was several years older than John and left home to get married when John was still a boy. All accounts suggest that Bill was never directly involved in the gang's activities. He did not rob banks, steal cars, or kill policemen. Still, violence was an enduring refrain in his life. During the course of one year, sheriff's deputies killed his brother John, his father, and his nephew Hanford Mobley. A couple years earlier, Robert Riblett, a Miami police officer, had killed Bill's brother Bob after Bob murdered Wilber Hendrickson, a jailer, in a failed attempt to free John Ashley from jail in Dade County. Hendrickson died in front of his wife in the doorway of their Miami home. Riblett, the police officer who stopped Bob Ashley, also died in the incident. Bill's two other brothers, Frank and Ed, were lost at sea while running illegal liquor from Bimini. His sister Daisy committed suicide a couple of years after John died by taking mercury bichloride tablets. And there is more. In an interview with Ada Williams, Frank Shore, DeSoto Tiger's brother-in-law, described the trust and close friendship Bill shared with the Seminoles. In fact, Shore goes on to say, that friendship was the only reason the Seminole men welcomed John into their camp that fateful winter in 1911.[3] It is the culmination of this tragic violence and the landscape's welcoming isolation that the Bill Ashley Jungles memorializes.

During the early 1930s Glen Simmons spent six months hunting with Wesley Mobley, Bill and John Ashley's brother-in-law and the father of Hanford Mobley, the Ashleys' young nephew who died at the Sebastian River bridge shootout. Simmons and Mobley were camping at a site on the Joe River named the Bill Ashley Camp in the Bill Ashley Jungles. A nostalgia for the Everglades that existed before the establishment of the national park has always been a theme of Simmons's stories. Yet this yearning was strongest when he talked about his time with Mobley at the Bill Ashley Camp. The Everglades of the Bill Ashley Jungles was a place where people suffering through hard times could escape their personal tragedies and where silence about those tragedies was expected. Simmons recalled Mobley staring into the campfire late into the evenings, and Simmons knew not to say a word. At the time Simmons was in his early teens, awed by the chance to spend time in the backcountry with a respected gladesman like Mobley.

On this particular trip, the men were pole-hunting, walking the Joe River marsh searching for alligators. They would leave camp in the morning, splitting up the marsh with Simmons going in one direction and Mobley in another. Apparently, at the end of the day, Simmons had the habit of walking the last half mile back to camp on Mobley's trail. Though Mobley never said much about it, Simmons said he knew that Mobley did not approve of this double tracking. One evening, as Simmons was heading back to camp along Mobley's trail, he came upon the drag marks made by the tail of a mid-sized alligator. Simmons became scared when he could not find any sign of alligator footprints along the drag line. As he said, "Everyone that ever

knocked around in the lower swamps has heard of large snakes hereabouts."
That night, Simmons tentatively asked Mobley if he had ever come across
any of those fantastic snakes. When Mobley replied by asking him if he had
ever seen any sign of one, Simmons knew he had been tricked. After that
Simmons stayed off Mobley's trail. Years later someone told him that Mobley had made the sign of the snake by hauling a large log across the trail.

Like the Ashley Gang, unnaturally large snakes appear throughout the
Everglades landscape. As Simmons's story suggests, these fantastic snakes had
the power to alter the landscape practices of humans—and perhaps of nonhumans too. In the late 1800s, such snakes seemed to roam freely throughout
southern Florida. Over the years, though, their range became narrower and
narrower, eventually moving closer and closer to the Bill Ashley Jungles. By
the time Simmons camped there, only the remote southern swamps, one of
the last areas "known" to outsiders, retained their reputation for serpentry.
I asked Simmons where the snake stories came from. He replied that somebody probably made them up to "discourage competition." He is probably
right, and perhaps the snake stories may have discouraged more than just
another hunter bent on following someone else's trail.

A decade after Simmons was dodging large snakes in the Bill Ashley
Jungles, President Harry S. Truman and other dignitaries gathered at the
fishing village of Chokoloskee, also along the mangrove coast, to celebrate
the establishment of Everglades National Park. In the years following that
celebration, Chokoloskee natives responded to the park's increasing hunting
and fishing restrictions by poaching alligators, hunting deer and other game
out of season, smuggling marijuana, damaging park property, and throwing
rocks and other debris at park employees. A few years later, national park
employees, citing mission and management concerns, forced residents of
Flamingo, the closest settlement to the Bill Ashley Jungles, from their homes
and then razed the remaining structures, compounding local animosity. Many
things are lost in the displacement of people from the places that define who
they are in the world. What was lost in this case is the Bill Ashley Jungles and
the snakes that kept outsiders at bay.

Yet mythic snakes have resurfaced to entangle our own time. Today Bur-
mese pythons, exotic imports released into the swamps of southern Florida,
roam the Everglades by the thousands. One of the world's largest snakes,

pythons can grow to over fifteen feet long and can weigh hundreds of pounds. In the Everglades, pythons captivate visitors, particularly when engaged in televised combat with alligators. The pythons' claims to the landscape have frustrated the efforts of resource managers, efforts that have included training a python-sniffing beagle and unleashing radio-transmitting decoy pythons into the Everglades. These snakes have returned to populate the Bill Ashley Jungles. I am hopeful that other aspects of the hunter's landscape can be reanimated as well.

NOTES

1. THE FLORIDA EVERGLADES

1. Ann Vileisis, *Discovering the Unknown Landscape: A History of America's Wetlands* (Washington, D.C.: Island Press, 1997).

2. See Bruce Braun, *The Intemperate Rain Forest* (Minneapolis: University of Minnesota Press, 2002); Joe Hermer, *Regulating Eden: The Nature of Order in North American Parks* (Toronto: University of Toronto Press, 2002); Karl Jacoby, *Crimes against Nature: Squatters, Poachers, Thieves, and the Hidden History of American Conservation* (Berkeley and Los Angeles: University of California Press, 2001); Mark D. Spence, *Dispossessing the Wilderness: Indian Removal and the Making of the National Parks* (New York: Oxford University Press, 1999); Roderick P. Neumann, *Imposing Wilderness: Struggles over Livelihood and Nature Preservation in Africa* (Berkeley and Los Angeles: University of California Press, 1998); William Cronon, "The Trouble with Wilderness; or, Getting Back to the Wrong Nature," in *Uncommon Ground: Toward Reinventing Nature,* ed. William Cronon (New York: W. W. Norton, 1995), 69–90; and Raymond Williams, "Ideas of Nature," in *Problems in Materialism and Culture* (London: Verso, 1980), 67–85.

3. Candace Slater, "Amazonia as Edenic Narrative," in Cronon, *Uncommon Ground,* 114–31.

4. Glen Simmons and Laura Ogden, *Gladesmen: Gator Hunters, Moonshiners, and Skiffers* (Gainesville: University of Florida Press, 1998).

5. U.S. Government Accountability Office (USGAO), *South Florida Ecosystem Restoration Is Moving Forward but Is Facing Significant Delays, Implementation Challenges, and Rising Costs* (Washington, D.C.: USGAO, 2007).

6. See Charles Redman, Morgan J. Grove, and Lauren H. Kuby, "Integrating Social Science into the Long-Term Ecological Research (LTER) Network: Social Dimensions of Ecological Change and Ecological Dimensions of Social Change," *Ecosystems* 7 (2004): 161–71; Sven Eric Jørgensen and Felix Muller, eds., *Handbook of Ecosystem Theories and Management* (Boca Raton, Fla.: Lewis Publishers, 2000);

Fikret Berkes and Carl Folke, *Linking Social and Ecological Systems: Management Practices and Social Mechanisms for Building Resilience* (Cambridge: Cambridge University Press, 1998); Frank B. Golley, *A History of the Ecosystem Concept in Ecology: More Than the Sum of the Parts* (New Haven: Yale University Press, 1993); and Emilio F. Moran, "Ecosystem Ecology in Biology and Anthropology: A Critical Assessment," in *The Ecosystem Approach in Anthropology,* ed. Emilio F. Moran (Ann Arbor: University of Michigan Press, 1990), 3–40.

7. Laura Ogden, "The Everglades Ecosystem and the Politics of Nature," *American Anthropologist* 110, no. 1 (2008): 21–32.

8. Patricia C. Griffin, ed., *Fifty Years of Southeastern Archaeology: Selected Works of John W. Griffin* (Gainesville: University Press of Florida, 1996).

9. John E. Worth, "Fontaneda Revisited: Five Descriptions of Sixteenth-Century Florida," *Florida Historical Quarterly* 73, no. 3 (1995): 339–52.

10. Griffin, *Fifty Years of Southeastern Archaeology.*

11. Jerald T. Milanich, *Laboring in the Fields of the Lord: Spanish Missions and Southeastern Indians* (Washington, D.C.: Smithsonian Institution Press, 1999).

12. Lucy L. Wenhold, ed. and trans., "A Seventeenth-Century Letter of Gabriel Díaz Vara Calderón, Bishop of Cuba," *Smithsonian Miscellaneous Collections* 95, no. 16 (1936): 1–14, 11–12.

13. Griffin, *Fifty Years of Southeastern Archaeology,* 201.

14. William C. Sturtevant and Jessica R. Cattelino, "Florida Seminole and Miccosukee," in *Handbook of North American Indians,* ed. William C. Sturtevant, vol. 14, *Southeast,* ed. Raymond D. Fogelson (Washington, D.C.: Smithsonian Institution Press, 2004), 429–49.

15. See Griffin, *Fifty Years of Southeastern Archaeology*; and Kenneth W. Porter, ed., *The Black Seminoles: History of a Freedom-Seeking People* (Gainesville: University Press of Florida, 1996).

16. James W. Covington, *The Seminoles of Florida* (Gainesville: University Press of Florida, 1993).

17. Griffin, *Fifty Years of Southeastern Archaeology,* 206.

18. *St. Augustine Weekly News,* January 8, 1841, "Notes on the Passages across the Everglades," in John M. Goggin Papers, George A. Smathers Libraries, University of Florida, Gainesville.

19. Charlton W. Tebeau, *Man in the Everglades: 2000 Years of Human History in the Everglades National Park* (Coral Gables, Fla.: University of Miami Press, 1968), 167.

20. John Titcomb Sprague, *The Origin, Progress, and Conclusion of the Florida War,* facs. reprod. of the 1848 edition, intro. John K. Mahon (Gainesville: University of Florida Press, 1969), 243–46.

21. *St. Augustine Weekly News,* January 8, 1841.

22. Ibid.

23. Griffin, *Fifty Years of Southeastern Archaeology.*

24. Harry A. Kersey, *Pelts, Plumes, and Hides: White Traders among the Seminole Indians, 1870–1930* (Gainesville: University Press of Florida, 1975), vi.

25. Ibid.

26. In spite of the nineteenth century's wars of removal, as well as the continued pressure by white settlers on land and game during the early part of the twentieth century, Florida Seminoles successfully maintained their cultural, economic, and political sovereignty. In 1962, some Florida Seminoles formed their own tribal organization and adopted the name "Miccosukee" to distinguish themselves politically from Seminoles who had sought federal reorganization in 1958 (Sturtevant and Cattelino, *Florida Seminole and Miccosukee*). The majority of the Seminoles are members of the Seminole Tribe of Florida (2,800 members in 2003), though in addition to the Miccosukee Tribe of Indians of Florida (600 members in 2004), there are dozens of families of Independent Seminole living near Naples, Florida, who refused federal recognition (ibid.). Today Seminoles and Miccosukees live in multiple reservations and communities throughout southern Florida in both rural and urban areas. There are major Seminole reservations at Brighton, Big Cypress, and Hollywood, and the majority of Miccosukees live within the Tamiami Trail Reservation area (ibid.). In addition to hunting (the traditional occupation), the tourist industry — from demonstrating alligator wrestling to selling handmade crafts — has been important to Seminole and Miccosukee people since the turn of the last century. Patsy West, *The Enduring Seminoles: From Alligator Wrestling to Ecotourism* (Gainesville: University Press of Florida, 1998). Wealth from casino operations has brought both the Seminole and Miccosukee tribes political power and economic independence, enabling them to support a myriad of social and cultural programs, as well as to build schools, health clinics, office complexes, and tribal housing. Jessica R. Cattelino, *High Stakes: Florida Seminole Gaming and Sovereignty* (Durham, N.C.: Duke University Press, 2008). The tribes have been able to leverage this economic and political power to substantially shape the direction of Everglades restoration initiatives.

27. Charles Vignoles, *The History of the Floridas, from the Discovery by Cabot, in 1497, to the Cession of the Same to the United States, in 1821. With Observations on the Climate, Soil, and Productions* (Brooklyn, N.Y.: Printed by G. L. Birch, 1824).

28. Archie P. Williams, "North to South through the Glades in 1883: The Account of the Second Expedition into the Florida Everglades by the *New Orleans Times-Democrat*," part 2, ed. Mary K. Wintringham, *Tequesta* 24 (1964): 77–78.

29. There are two types of tree islands within the Everglades. Thomas Lodge distinguishes them as upland tree islands, which are dominated by species that grow above sea level, such as red bay, sweet bay, willow, or cypress, and hammocks, which are found in the southern Everglades and are characterized by tropical hardwood trees, such as royal palm and cabbage palms, gumbo limbo, mahogany, strangler fig, poisonwood, and wild coffee. Lodge, *The Everglades Handbook: Understanding the Ecosystem* (Delray Beach, Fla.: St. Lucie Press, 1998).

30. Vileisis, *Discovering the Unknown Landscape.*

31. See David McCally, *The Everglades: An Environmental History* (Gainesville: University Press of Florida, 1999); and Stephen S. Light and Walter Dineen, "Water Control in the Everglades: A Historical Perspective," in *Everglades: The Ecosystem and Its Restoration,* ed. Steven M. Davis and John C. Ogden (Delray Beach, Fla.: St. Lucie Press, 1994), 47–84.

32. McCally, *The Everglades,* 59.

33. Walter Waldin, *Truck Farming in the Everglades* (Self-published, 1910), 12.

34. Okeechobee Fruit Lands Company, *The Garden in the Glades* (Jacksonville, Fla.: Okeechobee Fruit Lands Company, 1914), 2–3, emphasis added.

35. McCally, *The Everglades.*

36. Paul S. George, "Brokers, Binders, and Builders: Greater Miami's Boom of the Mid-1920s," *Florida Historical Quarterly* 65, no. 1 (1986): 27–51, 35.

37. Ibid., 30.

38. Lawrence Will, *Okeechobee Hurricane and the Hoover Dike* (Belle Glade, Fla.: Glades Historical Society, 1978).

39. Ibid.

40. John C. Ogden, "A Comparison of Wading Bird Nesting Colony Dynamics (1931–1946 and 1974–1989) as an Indication of Ecosystem Conditions in the Southern Everglades," in Davis and Ogden, *Everglades,* 533–70.

41. Gail Hollander, *Raising Cane in the 'Glades: The Global Sugar Trade and the Transformation of Florida* (Chicago: University of Chicago Press, 2008).

42. Marjory Stoneman Douglas, *The Everglades: River of Grass* (St. Simons Island, Ga.: Mockingbird Books, 1974). See also John Kunkel Small, *From Eden to Sahara: Florida's Tragedy* (Lancaster, Pa.: Science Press, 1929); and Charles Torrey Simpson, *Out of Doors in Florida: The Adventures of a Naturalist, together with Essays on the Wild Life and the Geology of the State* (Miami: E. B. Douglas, 1923).

43. John S. Lamb Sr., letter written to Tom Martin, manager of the Loxahatchee National Wildlife Refuge (undated; mid-1970s).

44. See, for example, Alden H. Hadley, "Reminiscences of the Florida Everglades," *Florida Naturalist* 14, no. 2 (1941): 21–22; John Whipple Potter Jenks, *Hunting*

in Florida in 1874 (Self-published, 1884); A. W. Dimock and J. Dimock, *Florida Enchantments* (New York: Outing Publishing, 1908).

45. Ben Orlove, *Lines in the Water: Nature and Culture at Lake Titicaca* (Berkeley and Los Angeles: University of California Press, 2002), 48–57.

THE QUEEN OF THE EVERGLADES

1. Several sources were helpful in my account of the Ashley Gang story, particularly the work of Hix C. Stuart, *The Notorious Ashley Gang: A Saga of the King and Queen of the Everglades* (Stuart, Fla.: St. Lucie Printing Co., 1928); and Ada Coats Williams, *Florida's Ashley Gang* (Port Salerno, Fla.: Florida Classics Library, 1996). Stuart's work was based on information the author compiled during the time the gang was active in southern Florida. Stuart lived in the same region as the Ashley Gang, was acquainted with John Ashley, and interviewed John Ashley, Ashley's mother, family friends, and law enforcement officers for his manuscript. Over the years, little additional information has been added to the historical record that was not already documented in Stuart's quaint and somewhat melodramatic little book. The exception is Williams's *Florida's Ashley Gang.* In her research, Williams interviewed family members of John Ashley's first known victim, DeSoto Tiger, and a sheriff's deputy who was at the scene of Ashley's death. These interviews provide needed historical context and help dispel many unsubstantiated rumors.

2. Walter Benjamin, "N [Re the Theory of Knowledge, Theory of Progress]," in *Benjamin: Philosophy, Aesthetics, History,* ed. Gary Smith (Chicago: University of Chicago Press, 1989), 43.

2. LANDSCAPE ETHNOGRAPHY AND THE POLITICS OF NATURE

1. Walter Benjamin, "Theses on the Philosophy of History," in *Illuminations,* edited and with an introduction by Hannah Arendt (New York: Schocken Books, 1968), 255.

2. Edward S. Casey, "How to Get from Space to Place in a Fairly Short Stretch of Time: Phenomenological Prolegomena," in *Senses of Place,* ed. Steven Feld and Keith H. Basso (Santa Fe, N.M.: School of American Research Press, 1996), 13–52; Michael Taussig, "The Beach (a Fantasy)," in *Landscape and Power,* ed. W. J. T. Mitchell (Chicago: University of Chicago Press, 2002), 317–48; Fred Myers, *Pintupi County, Pintupi Self: Sentiment, Place, and Politics among Western Desert Aborigines* (Washington, D.C.: Smithsonian Institution Press, 1986); Keith Basso, "Wisdom Sits in Places: Notes on a Western Apache Landscape," in Feld and Basso, *Senses of Place,*

53–90; Setha M. Low, *Behind the Gates: Life, Security, and the Pursuit of Happiness in Fortress America* (New York: Routledge, 2003); Kathleen C. Stewart, "An Occupied Place," in Feld and Basso, *Senses of Place*, 137–66.

3. See James Fairhead and Melissa Leach, *Misreading the African Landscape: Society and Ecology in a Forest Savanna Mosaic* (Cambridge: Cambridge University Press, 1996); K. I. MacDonald, "Global Hunting Grounds: Power, Scale, and Ecology in the Negotiation of Conservation," *Cultural Geographies* 12, no. 3 (2005): 259–91; Roderick P. Neumann, "Ways of Seeing Africa: Colonial Recasting of African Society and Landscape in Serengeti National Park," *Ecumene* 2, no. 2 (1995): 149–69; Neumann, *Imposing Wilderness*; Neumann, "Nature-State-Territory: Toward a Critical Theorization of Conservation Enclosures," in *Liberation Ecologies*, ed. R. Peet and M. Watts (London: Routledge, 2004), 195–217; David Rossiter, "The Nature of Protest: Constructing the Spaces of British Columbia's Rainforests," in *Cultural Geographies* 11, no. 2 (2004): 139–64; Paige West, James Igoe, and Dan Brockington, "Parks and Peoples: The Social Impacts of Protected Areas," in *Annual Review of Anthropology*, ed. W. H. Durham and J. Hill (Palo Alto, Calif.: Annual Reviews, 2006), 251–77; and Tania Murray Li, *The Will to Improve: Governmentality, Development, and the Practice of Politics* (Durham, N.C.: Duke University Press, 2007).

4. See Tim Cresswell, "Theorizing Place," in *Mobilizing Place, Placing Mobility: The Politics of Representation in a Globalized World*, ed. T. Cresswell and G. Verstraete (Amsterdam: Rodopi, 2003), 11–32; James Fox, *The Poetic Power of Place: Comparative Perspectives on Austronesian Ideas of Locality* (Canberra: Department of Anthropology with the Comparative Austronesian Project Research School of Pacific and Asian Studies, Australian National University, 1997); Amy Mills, "Boundaries of the Nation in the Space of the Urban: Landscape and Social Memory in Istanbul," *Cultural Geographies* 13, no. 3 (2006): 367–94; Donald Moore, "Subaltern Struggles and the Politics of Place: Remapping Resistance in Zimbabwe's Eastern Highlands," *Cultural Anthropology* 13, no. 3 (1998): 344–81; Edward Said, "Invention, Memory, and Place," in Mitchell, *Landscape and Power*; Tom Selwyn, "Landscapes of Liberation and Imprisonment: Towards an Anthropology of the Israeli Landscape," in *The Anthropology of Landscape: Perspectives of Place and Space*, ed. E. Hirsch and M. O'Hanlon (Oxford: Clarendon Press, 1995), 114–34; and Daniel Trudeau, "Politics of Belonging in the Construction of Landscapes: Place-Making, Boundary-Drawing, and Exclusion," *Cultural Geographies* 13, no. 3 (2006): 421–43.

5. David Matless, "Introduction: The Properties of Landscape," in *Handbook of Cultural Geography*, ed. K. Anderson (London: Sage, 2003), 227–32.

6. Eric Hirsch, "Landscape: Between Place and Space," in Hirsch and O'Hanlon, *The Anthropology of Landscape*, 1–30.

7. Simon Schama, *Landscape and Memory* (New York: Alfred A. Knopf, 1995).

8. See for example, Eduardo Batalha Viveiros de Castro, "Exchanging Perspectives: The Transformation of Objects into Subjects in Amerindian Ontologies," *Common Knowledge* 10, no. 3 (2004): 463–84; and Eduardo Kohn, "How Dogs Dream: Amazonian Names and the Politics of Transspecies Engagement," *American Ethnologist* 34, no. 1 (2007): 3–24.

9. Bruno Latour, *We Have Never Been Modern,* trans. Catherine Porter (Cambridge, Mass.: Harvard University Press, 1993).

10. Donna Haraway, *When Species Meet* (Minneapolis: University of Minnesota Press, 2008).

11. Paul Robbins, *Lawn People: How Grasses, Weeds, and Chemicals Make Us Who We Are* (Philadelphia: Temple University Press, 2007).

12. Gilles Deleuze and Félix Guattari, "Introduction: Rhizome," in *A Thousand Plateaus: Capitalism and Schizophrenia,* translated and with a foreword by Brian Massumi (Minneapolis: University of Minnesota Press, 1987), 3–25; Deleuze and Guattari, *Kafka: Toward a Minor Literature,* trans. Dana Polan (Minneapolis: University of Minnesota Press, 1986); see also the discussion by Braun, *The Intemperate Rain Forest,* 265.

13. Peter Hogarth, *The Biology of Mangroves and Seagrasses* (Cambridge: Oxford University Press, 2007), 2.

14. See Herbert Keightley Job, *Wild Wings: Adventures of a Camera Hunter among the Larger Wild Birds of North America on Sea and Land* (Boston: Houghton Mifflin, 1905), 42; Charles Torrey Simpson, *In Lower Florida Wilds: A Naturalist's Observations on the Life, Physical Geography, and the Geology of the More Tropical Parts of the State* (New York: G. P. Putnam's Sons, 1920), 110; Louis A. Stimson, "Off the Map," *Florida Naturalist* 13, no. 4 (1940): 80–82; and Frank M. Chapman, *Camps and Cruises of an Ornithologist* (New York: D. Appleton, 1908), 140.

15. Deleuze and Guattari, *A Thousand Plateaus,* 293, 12.

16. Ibid., 12–13.

17. Ibid., 25.

18. Ibid., 21.

19. Bruno Latour, *Politics of Nature: How to Bring the Sciences into Democracy* (Cambridge, Mass.: Harvard University Press, 2004), 53.

20. Deleuze and Guattari, *A Thousand Plateaus,* 444.

21. Mark Bonta and John Proveti, *Deleuze and Geophilosophy: A Guide and Glossary* (Edinburgh: Edinburgh University Press, 2004), 52.

22. Philip Abrams, "Notes on the Difficulty of Studying the State (1977)," *Journal of Historical Sociology* 1, no. 1 (1988): 58–89; and James Scott, *Seeing Like the*

State: How Certain Schemes to Improve the Human Condition Have Failed (New Haven: Yale University Press, 1998). Tania Murray Li offers an important engagement with Scott's approach in "Beyond the 'State' and Failed Schemes," *American Anthropologist* 107, no. 3 (2005): 383–94; Donald S. Moore, in *Suffering for Territory: Race, Place, and Power in Zimbabwe* (Durham, N.C.: Duke University Press, 2005), extends Michel Foucault's framework of governmentality to help us understand the micropolitics and the limitations of state power.

23. See Fairhead and Leach, *Misreading the African Landscape*; Ramachandra Guha, *The Unquiet Woods: Ecological Change and Peasant Resistance in the Himalaya* (Delhi: Oxford University Press, 1989); Neumann, *Imposing Wilderness*; Neumann, "Nature-State-Territory"; Nancy Peluso, *Rich Forests, Poor People: Resource Control and Resistance in Java* (Berkeley and Los Angeles: University of California Press, 1992); and Peluso, "Weapons of the Wild: Strategic Uses of Violence and Wilderness in the Rain Forests of Indonesian Borneo," in *In Search of the Rain Forest,* ed. Candace Slater (Durham, N.C.: Duke University Press, 2003), 204–45.

24. Andrew Pickering, *The Mangle of Practice: Time, Agency, and Science* (Chicago: University of Chicago Press, 1995), 23.

25. Deleuze and Guattari, *Kafka,* 7.

THE NOTORIOUS ASHLEY GANG

1. Stuart, *The Notorious Ashley Gang,* 8.

2. Ibid., 65.

3. Williams, *Florida's Ashley Gang,* 8.

4. Seminole Tribe of Florida, "Indian Murder Launches Criminal Career," *Seminole Tribune* 20, no. 43 (July 30, 1993).

5. Oren B. Padgett, "Personal Recollections of Oren Benton 'O. B.' Padgett," in *O. B. Padgett: The Native Son, the Lawman, the Prisoner, the Citizen,* ed. Alice L. Luckhardt (Stuart, Fla.: Alice L. Luckhardt, 2008), 33.

6. Stuart, *The Notorious Ashley Gang,* 65–66.

3. EARTH, FIRE, AND FLESH

1. Susan Buck-Morss, *Dreamworld and Catastrophe: The Passing of Mass Utopia in East and West* (Cambridge: MIT Press, 2002), 101.

2. Roland Barthes, *A Lover's Discourse: Fragments* (New York: Hill and Wang, 1978).

3. Ibid., 4.

4. Ibid., 232.

5. Deleuze and Guattari, *A Thousand Plateaus,* 323.

6. Ibid., 313.

7. Bonta and Protevi, *Deleuze and Geophilosophy,* 349.

8. Bruce Braun, "Environmental Issues: Inventive Life," *Progress in Human Geography* 32, no. 5 (2008): 667–79.

9. Deleuze and Guattari, *A Thousand Plateaus,* 312, emphasis added.

10. Connie Toops, *The Alligator: Monarch of the Marsh,* 2nd ed. (Homestead, Fla.: Parks and Monuments Association, 1988).

11. Daphne Soares, "Neurology: An Ancient Sensory Organ in Crocodilians," *Nature,* May 16, 2002, 241–42.

12. Frank Craighead Sr., "The Role of the Alligator in Shaping Plant Communities and Maintaining Wildlife in the Southern Everglades," *Florida Naturalist* 41 (1968): 2–7, 69–74, 94.

13. Ibid.

14. See David Alderton, *Crocodiles and Alligators of the World* (London: Blandford, 1991), 33; Vaughn L. Glasgow, *A Social History of the American Alligator* (New York: St. Martin's Press, 1991), 28; and Charles B. Cory, *Hunting and Fishing in Florida, Including a Key to the Water Birds Known to Occur in the State* (Boston: Estes and Lauriat, 1896), 69.

15. LeRoy Overstreet, "Memories of Gator Hunts," in *Alligators: Prehistoric Presence in the American Landscape,* ed. Martha A. Strawn (Baltimore: The Johns Hopkins University Press, 1997), 33–109, 36.

16. Overstreet, "Memories of Gator Hunts," 48.

17. Stephen J. Pyne, *Fire: A Brief History* (Seattle: University of Washington Press, 2001), 46.

18. Franz Boas, *The Mind of a Primitive Man* (New York: Macmillan, 1938), 156.

19. William B. Robertson, "Everglades Fires — Past, Present, and Future," *Everglades Natural History* 2, no. 1 (1954): 9–16, 16.

20. Glasgow, *A Social History of the American Alligator.*

21. Simmons and Ogden, *Gladesmen,* 98.

22. Dimock and Dimock, *Florida Enchantments,* 116.

23. Cory, *Hunting and Fishing in Florida,* 66.

24. Kohn, "How Dogs Dream," 3–24, 18.

25. Munroe, quoted in Kevin M. McCarthy, *Alligator Tales* (Sarasota, Fla.: Pineapple Press, 1998), 67.

26. Simmons and Ogden, *Gladesmen,* 103.

27. Michael Taussig, *Mimesis and Alterity: A Particular History of the Senses* (New York: Routledge, 1993), xiii.

28. Deleuze and Guattari, *Kafka,* 13.

29. Deleuze and Guattari, *A Thousand Plateaus,* 313.

30. Bartram, quoted in Glasgow, *A Social History of the American Alligator,* 19.

31. Van Campen Heilner, *Adventures in Angling: A Book of Salt Water Fishing* (Cincinnati, Ohio: Stewart Kidd, 1922).

32. Ibid., 208.

33. Gilles Deleuze and Félix Guattari, *What Is Philosophy?* trans. Hugh Tomlinson and Graham Burchell (New York: Columbia University Press, 1994).

THE THEATRICS OF EVERGLADES OUTLAWS

1. Stuart, *The Notorious Ashley Gang,* 10.

2. Williams, *Florida's Ashley Gang,* 13.

3. Ibid., 41.

4. Stuart, *The Notorious Ashley Gang,* 28.

5. Ibid., 22.

6. Ibid., 23.

7. Ibid.

4. THE TRAVELS OF SNAKES, MANGROVES, AND MEN

1. Susan Sontag, foreword to Robert Walser, *Selected Stories* (New York: Vintage Press, 1983), viii.

2. Benjamin Kunkel, "Still Small Voice: The Fiction of Robert Walser," *New Yorker,* August 6, 2007.

3. Walter Benjamin, "Robert Walser," in *Robert Walser Rediscovered: Stories, Fairy-Tale Plays, and Critical Responses,* ed. Mark Harman (Hanover, N.H.: Published for Dartmouth College by University Press of New England, 1985), 144.

4. Deleuze and Guattari, *A Thousand Plateaus,* 88–89.

5. Barbara Bender, "Time and Landscape," *Current Anthropology,* Supplement 43 (2002): S103–S112, S103.

6. Tim Cresswell, *On the Move: Mobility in the Modern Western World* (New York: Routledge, 2006), 3.

7. Susan Buck-Morss, *The Dialectics of Seeing* (Cambridge: MIT Press, 1991), 304.

8. Taussig, *Mimesis and Alterity.*

9. Latour, *We Have Never Been Modern.*

10. Braun, *The Intemperate Rain Forest.*

11. Robert Walser, *"Masquerade," and Other Stories* (Baltimore: The John Hopkins University Press, 1990), 33.

12. Douglas, *The Everglades,* 1.

13. Hugh Willoughby, *Across the Everglades: A Canoe Journey of Exploration* (Port Salerno, Fla.: Florida Classics Library, 1992), 110.

14. Henri Lefebvre, *The Production of Space* (Oxford: Basil Blackwell, 1984), 95–96.

15. Marilyn Nissenson and Susan Jonas, *Snake Charm* (New York: Harry N. Abrams, 1995), 19.

16. Weston La Barre, *They Shall Take Up Serpents: Psychology of the Southern Snake-Handling Cult* (Prospect Heights, Ill.: Waveland Press, 1969).

17. E. O. Wilson, *In Search of Nature* (Washington D.C.: Island Press, 1996), 5.

18. "Got a Snake in His Net," *Miami Metropolis* 2, no. 17 (March 5, 1897): 18.

19. "Capture of a Big Python," *New York Times,* March 7, 1897.

20. Archie P. Williams, "North to South through the Glades in 1883: The Account of the Second Expedition into the Florida Everglades by the *New Orleans Times-Democrat,*" part 1, ed. Mary K. Wintringham, *Tequesta* 23 (1963): 33–59, 45.

21. Tebeau, *Man in the Everglades.*

22. James A. Henshall, *Camping and Cruising in Florida* (Cincinnati, Ohio: Robert Clarke, 1884), 190.

23. "A Trip in the Glades: What a Party of Buena Vista People Saw and Did on a Recent Trip in the Long Key Country of the Glades," *Miami Metropolis* 1, no. 10 (July 17, 1896): 6.

24. Willoughby, *Across the Everglades,* 88.

25. Roberts, quoted in K. A. Bickel, *The Mangrove Coast: The Story of the West Coast of Florida* (New York: Coward-McCann, 1942), 233.

26. Barthes, *A Lover's Discourse.*

27. Willoughby, *Across the Everglades,* 37.

28. Simmons and Ogden, *Gladesmen,* 55.

29. Schama, *Landscape and Memory,* 7.

30. Christopher Tilley, *A Phenomenology of Landscape: Places, Paths, and Monuments* (Oxford: Berg, 1995), 28. Tilley discusses the ways in which human experience and memory become inscribed upon a landscape, saying, "Daily passages through the landscape become biographic encounters for individuals, recalling traces of past activities and previous events and the reading of signs" (27). For Tilley, locations and landscapes are embedded with social and individual memory, and the process of moving through these landscapes involves the "continuous presencing of previous experiences in present contexts" (28).

31. Marc Augé, *In the Metro* (Minneapolis: University of Minnesota Press, 2002), 4.

32. Hogarth, *The Biology of Mangroves and Seagrasses*, 11.

33. See John H. Davis Jr., "The Ecology and Geologic Role of Mangroves in Florida," in *Papers from the Tortugas Laboratory of the Carnegie Institute of Washington*, vol. 32, publication no. 517 (Washington, D.C.: Carnegie Institution of Washington, 1940), 304–412; and Carl D. Monk, "The Tree That Walks on Stilts," *Everglades Natural History* 2, no. 3 (1954): 143–47.

34. Ariel E. Lugo, "Mangrove Ecosystems: Successional or Steady State?" *Biotropica* 12, no. 2 (1980): 65–72.

35. Hogarth, *The Biology of Mangroves and Seagrasses*, 11.

36. Chapman, *Camps and Cruises of an Ornithologist*, 140.

37. Deleuze and Guattari, *Kafka*, 7.

THE GANG VANISHES INTO THE MYSTERIOUS SWAMP

1. Padgett, quoted in Luckhardt, *O. B. Padgett*, 36.

5. SEARCHING FOR PARADISE IN THE FLORIDA EVERGLADES

1. Latour, *Politics of Nature*, 53.

2. N. Myers, "Threatened Biotas: 'Hot Spots' in Tropical Forests," *Environmentalist* 8, no. 3 (1988): 187–208.

3. Aldo A. Leopold, *Sand County Almanac and Sketches Here and There* (New York: Oxford University Press, 1949).

4. *Oxford English Dictionary on CD-ROM*, prepared by J. A. Simpson and E. S. C. Weiner (Oxford: Clarendon Press, 1989). See also Lodge, *The Everglades Handbook*.

5. R. H. Humes, "A Short History of Liguus Collecting: With a List of Collectors—1744 to 1958," *Tequesta* 25 (1965): 69–74.

6. W. S. Jennings, "Royal Palm State Park," *Tropic Magazine* 4 (1916): 10–26.

7. Ibid.

8. Neumann, *Imposing Wilderness*.

9. Spence, *Dispossessing the Wilderness*. See also West, Igoe, and Brockington, "Parks and Peoples," 251–77; and Jacoby, *Crimes against Nature*.

10. Jackson, quoted in J. C. Taylor, "Introduction to Railway Location in the Florida Everglades, by William J. Krome," *Tequesta* 39 (1979): 5–7.

11. Braun, *The Intemperate Rain Forest*, 26–57.

12. James Clifford, *The Predicament of Culture: Twentieth-Century Ethnography, Literature, and Art* (Cambridge, Mass.: Harvard University Press, 1988); see also C. M. Hinsley, *Savages and Scientists: The Smithsonian Institute and the Development of American Anthropology, 1846–1910* (Washington, D.C.: Smithsonian Institution Press, 1981).

13. W. E. Safford, "Natural History of Paradise Key and the Nearby Everglades of Florida," in *Annual Report of the Board of Regents of the Smithsonian Institution: 1917* (Washington, D.C.: Smithsonian Institution, 1919).

14. Latour, *Politics of Nature,* 22.

15. Paige West and J. G. Carrier, "Getting Away from It All? Ecotourism and Authenticity," *Current Anthropology* 45, no. 4 (2004): 483–98; see also West, Igoe, and Brockington, *Parks and Peoples,* 261.

16. Robert Kohler, *All Creatures: Naturalists, Collectors, and Biodiversity, 1850–1950* (Princeton: Princeton University Press, 2006).

17. Latour, *Politics of Nature,* 22.

18. Daniel B. Beard, *Wildlife Reconnaissance: Everglades National Park Project* (Washington, D.C.: National Park Service, 1938).

19. Willoughby, *Across the Everglades,* 13.

20. Ibid., 64.

21. Ibid.

22. Dimock and Dimock, *Florida Enchantments,* 217.

23. C. S. "Ted" Smallwood, "Reminiscences of Charles Sherod 'Ted' Smallwood," in *The Story of the Chokoloskee Bay Country,* ed. Charlton W. Tebeau (Coral Gables, Fla.: University of Miami Press, 1968), 84.

24. "A Trip in the Glades," 6.

25. Willoughby, *Across the Everglades,* 64.

26. Willoughby used the term "Long Key" (*Across the Everglades,* 64), but it is called Long Pine Key today.

27. See Vladimir Nabokov, *Strong Opinions* (New York: McGraw-Hill, 1973); and Nabokov, *Speak, Memory: An Autobiography Revisited* (New York: Vintage Press, 1989).

28. Leah La Plante, "The Sage of Biscayne Bay: Charles Torrey Simpson's Love Affair with South Florida," *Tequesta* 47 (1995): 61–82, 64.

29. Simpson, quoted in ibid., 61

30. John Kunkel Small, "Royal Palm Hammock," *Journal of the New York Botanical Garden* 17 (October 1916): 165–72.

31. Munroe, quoted in ibid., 167.

32. Francis and John Soar, quoted in Small, "Royal Palm Hammock," 167.

33. Thelma Peters, *Lemon City: Pioneering on Biscayne Bay, 1850–1925* (Miami, Fla.: Banyan Books, 1976), 179.

34. Small, "Royal Palm Hammock," 166.

35. Simpson, *Out of Doors in Florida,* 251–52.

36. Charles Torrey Simpson, "Paradise Key," *Tropic Magazine* 4 (1916): 5–9; see also Thomas Barbour, *That Vanishing Eden: A Naturalist's Florida* (Boston: Little, Brown, 1944), 162.

37. Frank M. Chapman, "Everglades Islet," *Audubon Magazine* 45, no. 1 (1943): 19–25.

38. Arthur Howell, "A List of the Birds of Royal Palm Hammock, Florida," *Auk* 38 (April 1921): 250–63, 251.

39. Small, "Royal Palm Hammock," 168; see also Elizabeth Ogren Rothra, *Florida's Pioneer Naturalist: The Life of Charles Torrey Simpson* (Gainesville: University Press of Florida, 1995), 85.

40. Simpson, *In Lower Florida Wilds,* 130–33; see also Rothra, *Florida's Pioneer Naturalist,* 84–85.

41. Simpson, *In Lower Florida Wilds,* 130–33.

42. Safford, "Natural History of Paradise Key and the Nearby Everglades of Florida," 377.

43. Arthur Howell, *Florida Bird Life* (New York: Coward-McCann, 1932), 252.

44. See John Kunkel Small, "Exploration in Southern Florida in 1915," *Journal of the New York Botanical Garden* 17 (March 1916): 37–45, 38; Small, "Coastwise Dunes and Lagoons: A Record of Botanical Exploration in Florida in the Spring of 1918," *Journal of the New York Botanical Garden* 20 (1919): 191–207; and Small, "Royal Palm Hammock."

45. David Arnold, *The Problem of Nature: Environment, Culture, and European Expansion* (Oxford: Basil Blackwell, 1996), 143.

46. Safford, "Natural History of Paradise Key and the Nearby Everglades of Florida," 377.

47. See Mary Louise Pratt, *Imperial Eyes: Travel Writing and Transculturation* (London: Routledge, 1992).

48. Kohler, *All Creatures,* 8.

49. Ibid., 18.

50. Ibid., 157–61.

51. See Simmons and Ogden, *Gladesmen*; and Kersey, *Pelts, Plumes, and Hides.*

52. Beard, *Wildlife Reconnaissance,* 84–85.

53. John Kunkel Small, "The Royal Palm—Roystonea Regia," *Journal of the New York Botanical Garden* 29 (1928): 1–9, 1.

54. See *State Library Bulletin*, vol. 1 (Albany: State University of New York, 1899), 592; Office of the Publishers' Weekly, *The Annual American* (New York: R. R. Bowker, 1898); and F. F. Brown and W. R. Brown, eds., *Dial: A Semi-Monthly Journal of Literary Criticism, Discussion, and Information* 24 (March 1898): 186–88.

55. Small, "Exploration in Southern Florida in 1915," 37.

56. Simpson, *Out of Doors in Florida*, 137; see also Simpson, *In Lower Florida Wilds*, 141.

57. See Small, "Exploration in Southern Florida in 1915," 41; and Small, "Royal Palm Hammock," 170.

58. "A Trip in the Glades."

59. Small, "Royal Palm Hammock," 167.

60. Simpson, *Out of Doors in Florida*, 381.

61. Kohler, *All Creatures*, 18.

62. Jacoby, *Crimes against Nature*.

63. Jennings, "Royal Palm State Park," 10.

64. See Simpson, *Out of Doors in Florida*, 243; and "A Trip in the Glades."

65. Jennings, "Royal Palm State Park."

66. See Small, "Royal Palm Hammock," 9; and Simpson, "Paradise Key," 6–7.

67. Simpson, "Paradise Key."

68. Latour, *Politics of Nature*, 22.

69. Hermer, *Regulating Eden*, 114–15.

6. ALLIGATOR CONSERVATION, COMMODITIES, AND TACTICS OF SUBVERSION

1. See W. Scott Prudham, *Knock on Wood: Nature as Commodity in Douglas-Fir Country* (New York: Routledge, 2005); Philippe Le Billon, "The Geopolitical Economy of 'Resource Wars,'" *Geopolitics* 9, no. 1 (2004): 1–28; and Noel Castree, "Commodifying What Nature?" *Progress in Human Geography* 27, no. 3 (2003): 273–97.

2. Castree, "Commodifying What Nature?" 281.

3. Jacoby, *Crimes against Nature*, 2.

4. See Serena Rasmussen and Manoj Shivlani, "The Alligator: A History of Slaughter, Recovery, Current Protection, and Future Conservation," in *Urban Growth and Sustainable Habitats: Case Studies of Policy Conflict in South Florida's Coastal Environment*, ed. D. Suman, M. Shivlani, and M. Villanueva (Miami: Division of Marine Affairs and Policy, Rosenstiel School of Marine and Atmospheric Science, 1995), 92–109; and Toops, *The Alligator*.

5. Kevin M. McCarthy, *Alligator Tales* (Sarasota, Fla.: Pineapple Press, 1998), 57.

6. John Thorbjarnarson, "Crocodile Tears and Skins: International Trade, Economic Constraints, and Limits to the Sustainable Use of Crocodilians," *Conservation Biology* 13, no. 3 (1999): 465–70, 465.

7. Alderton, *Crocodiles and Alligators of the World*, 33.

8. Karlheinz H. P. Fuchs, Charles A. Ross, A. C. Pooley, and Romulus Whitaker, "Crocodile-Skin Products," in *Crocodiles and Alligators*, ed. Charles A. Ross (New York: Facts on File, 1989), 188–95, 188.

9. W. I. Drysdale and F. C. Usina, "Gator . . . Saint or Sinner?" *Florida Wildlife* 1, no. 4 (1947): 3–10.

10. Fuchs et al., "Crocodile-Skin Products."

11. Albert Reese, *The Alligator and Its Allies* (New York: G. P. Putnam's Sons, 1915), 28.

12. P. Brazaitis, "The Trade in Crocodilians," in Ross, *Crocodiles and Alligators*, 196–201.

13. Kevin R. Van Jaarsveldt, "Flaying, Curing, and Measuring Crocodile Skins," in *Wildlife Management: Crocodiles and Alligators*, ed. S. Charlie Manolis, Grahame J. W. Webb, and Peter J. Whitehead (Chipping Norton, Australia: Surrey Beatty and Sons, 1987), 387–92.

14. Reese, *The Alligator and Its Allies*, 28.

15. Dimock and Dimock, *Florida Enchantments*, 119.

16. Kersey, *Pelts, Plumes, and Hides*, 127.

17. Florida Department of Game and Fresh Water Fish, *First Annual Report* (Tallahassee, Fla.: T. J. Appleyard, State Printer, 1914). In 1935, the Florida Department of Game and Fresh Water Fish became the Florida Game and Fresh Water Fish Commission (FGFC). In 1999, the FGFC was combined with the Florida Marine Patrol, becoming the Florida Fish and Wildlife Conservation Commission.

18. Jane Gibson-Carpenter, "Skin and Bones: Politics and Consequences of Natural Resource Management in Shellcracker Haven, Florida, by the Florida Game and Fresh Water Fish Commission" (Ph.D. diss., University of Florida, 1992).

19. Vileisis, *Discovering the Unknown Landscape*.

20. Robert Walker and William Solecki, "Theorizing Land-Cover and Land-Use Change: The Case of the Florida Everglades and Its Degradation," *Annals of the Association of American Geographers* 94, no. 2 (2004): 311–28.

21. Ibid.; see also McCally, *The Everglades*.

22. *Florida: A Guide to the Southernmost State*, American Guide Series, compiled and written by the Federal Writers' Project of the Work Projects Administration for the State of Florida in 1939. Reissued, with a new introduction by John I.

McCollum, as *The WPA Guide to Florida: The Federal Writers' Project Guide to 1930s Florida* (New York: Pantheon Books, 1984).

23. David Kadlec, "Zora Neale Hurston and the Federal Folk," MODERNISM/ *modernity* 7, no. 3 (2000): 471–85, 473.

24. Gary R. Mormino, "On the Brink: Florida on the Eve of World War II," *Florida Humanities Council Forum* 21, no. 3 (1999): 12.

25. FGFC, *Biennial Report: Florida Game and Fresh Water Fish Commission, Biennium Ending December 31, 1936* (Tallahassee: FGFC, 1937), 28.

26. FGFC, *Biennial Report: Florida Game and Fresh Water Fish Commission, Biennium Ending December 31, 1938* (Tallahassee: FGFC, 1939), 22.

27. FGFC, *Biennial Report: Florida Game and Fresh Water Fish Commission, Biennium Ending December 31, 1940* (Tallahassee: FGFC, 1941), 22.

28. Florida House Bill 1839, signed in June 1939, banned alligator hunting in Dade County.

29. Walker and Solecki, "Theorizing Land-Cover and Land-Use Change."

30. James T. Huffstodt, *Everglades Lawmen: True Stories of Game Wardens in the Glades* (Sarasota, Fla.: Pineapple Press, 2000), viii.

31. See, for example, FGFC, *Biennial Report: Florida Game and Fresh Water Fish Commission, Biennium Ending December 31, 1948* (Tallahassee: FGFC, 1949).

32. Huffstodt, *Everglades Lawmen.*

33. "State Men Break Up Gator Poaching Ring," *Florida Wildlife* 2, no. 4 (1948): 21.

34. Huffstodt, *Everglades Lawmen.*

35. Maria Stone, *Dwellers of the Sawgrass and Sand: Natives and Near-Natives,* vol. 3 (Naples, Fla.: Butterfly Press, 1996), 94.

36. Le Billon, "The Geopolitical Economy of 'Resource Wars,'" 2.

37. See James Scott, *Weapons of the Weak: Everyday Forms of Peasant Resistance* (New Haven: Yale University Press, 1985); and Scott, *Domination and the Arts of Resistance: Hidden Transcripts* (New Haven: Yale University Press, 1990).

38. Neumann, *Imposing Wilderness,* 44–50.

39. Ibid., 49.

40. Raymond Williams, "Base and Superstructure in Marxist Cultural Theory," in *Rethinking Popular Culture: Contemporary Perspectives in Cultural Studies,* ed. Chandra Mukerji and Michael Schudson (Berkeley and Los Angeles: University of California Press, 1991), 407–23.

41. Wilfred T. Neill, *The Last of the Ruling Reptiles: Alligators, Crocodiles, and Their Kin* (New York: Columbia University Press, 1971), 261.

42. Drysdale and Usina, "Gator . . . Saint or Sinner?" 3.

43. Florida Game and Fresh Water Fish Commission, "Gator Conservation Committee Makes Management Suggestions," *Florida Wildlife* 3, no. 12 (1949): 22.

44. Dick Bothwell, *The Great Outdoors Book of Alligators and Other Crocodilia* (St. Petersburg, Fla.: Great Outdoors Publishing, 1962), 7.

45. Toops, *The Alligator*, 46.

46. Chesser, quoted in Stone, *Dwellers of the Sawgrass and Sand*, 93.

47. Allan R. Woodward, "American Alligators in Florida," in *Our Living Resources: A Report to the Nation on the Distribution, Abundance, and Health of US Plants, Animals, and Ecosystems*, ed. E. T. LaRoe (Washington, D.C.: U.S. Department of the Interior, National Biological Service, 1995), 127.

48. See F. J. Mazzotti and L. A. Brandt, "Ecology of the American Alligator in a Seasonally Fluctuating Environment," in Davis and Ogden, *Everglades*, 485–505; and Allan R. Woodward and Clinton T. Moore, *Statewide Alligator Surveys* (Tallahassee: Bureau of Wildlife Research, FGFC, 1990).

49. Storter, quoted in Andrew H. Brown, "Haunting Heart of the Everglades," *National Geographic* 93, no. 2 (1948): 147–73.

50. Woodward and Moore, *Statewide Alligator Surveys*.

51. Woodward, "American Alligators in Florida."

52. FGFC, *Florida Game and Fresh Water Fish Commission, Annual Report (July 1, 1976–June 30, 1977)* (Tallahassee: FGFC, 1977), 26.

53. T. C. Hines and H. F. Percival, "Alligator Management and Value-Added Conservation in Florida," in *Valuing Wildlife: Economic and Social Perspectives*, ed. D. J. Decker and G. R. Goff (Boulder, Colo.: Westview Press, 1987), 164–73.

54. See Gibson-Carpenter, "Skin and Bones," for further discussion.

55. E. P. Thompson, *Whigs and Hunters: The Origin of the Black Act* (New York: Pantheon Books, 1975); and Douglas Hay, "Poaching and the Game Laws on Cannock Chase," in *Albion's Fatal Tree: Crime and Society in Eighteenth Century England*, ed. Douglas Hay, Peter Linebaugh, John G. Rule, E. P. Thompson, and Cal Winslow (New York: Pantheon Books, 1975), 189–253.

56. Hay, "Poaching and the Game Laws on Cannock Chase," 189.

57. Beard, *Wildlife Reconnaissance*, 58.

58. Ibid., 86.

59. Reese, *The Alligator and Its Allies*, 10.

60. Simpson, *Out of Doors in Florida*, 137.

61. See McCally, *The Everglades*; and Light and Dineen, "Water Control in the Everglades," 47–84.

62. Mazzotti and Brandt, "Ecology of the American Alligator," 498.

63. Ibid.

EPILOGUE

1. Howard Jaffe, "Preliminary Report on a Midden Mound and Burial Mound of the Boynton Mound Complex," *Florida Anthropologist* 29, no. 4 (1976): 145–52.

2. Randall Hackley, "Wedding Bells Were Ringing for Prisoners as Early as 1925," *Miami Herald,* November 11, 1982.

3. Williams, *Florida's Ashley Gang,* 8.

INDEX

Barthes, Roland, 44–45, 83
Bartram, William, 66
Beard, Daniel, 149
Bender, Barbara, 74
Benjamin, Walter, 22, 74, 75
Bessey, Ernst, 109
Big Cypress Swamp, 8, 10, 65
Bill Ashley Camp, 155
Bill Ashley Jungles, 25–26, 28, 154, 157;
    as a rhizome, 29–30, 32–33; travel
    through, 83, 143
Bloxham, William, 12
Boas, Franz, 55
Bonta, Mark, 33, 45
Brandt, L. A., 150
Braun, Bruce, 45, 100
Brewer, Ed, 82, 103–7, 113, 116, 118
Britton, Nathan Lord, 109
Brooker, Ed, 87
Brown's Boat Landing, 10
Buck-Morss, Susan, 44, 75

Calderón, Gabriel Díaz Vara, 6
Calusas, 5–6, 101
Casey, Edward, 27
Castree, Noel, 125
Central and Southern Florida
    Project (C & SF Project), 14–17,
    135–36
Chapman, Frank M., 89–90
Chekika, 8–10
Chesser, Leonard, 147
Chokoloskee Island, 5, 10, 104
Chokoloskee natives, 156
Comprehensive Everglades Restora-
    tion Plan (CERP), 4
conservation policies, 2, 27, 100, 117,
    126, 131, 146; Everglades and, 4, 15,

95; water, 135; wildlife, 96, 132. *See
also alligator conservation
Corkscrew Swamp, 63, 143
Cory, Charles, 60
"crackers," 18
Craighead, Frank, Sr., 49
Cresswell, Tim, 74–75
critique, 26

Dawson, George Mercer, 100
Dead-Pecker Slough, 115
Deleuze, Gilles and Félix Guattari, 43,
    74, 90; "refrain," 45, 46, 47, 64;
    rhizome, 29–31, 35, 36; territoriality,
    66; view of the state, 33
Dimock, Anthony W., 58–59, 104, 129
Disston, Hamilton, 12
Douglas, Marjory Stoneman, 77
drainage, 12–17, 20, 149–50

earth, 32, 45–46, 46–50, 64, 126
Eaton, Alvah Augustus, 108
ecosystem management, 4
Ed Brooker's Landings, 87
Endangered Species Act, 147
ethnographic writing, 30
Everglades: American exploration of,
    8–11, 81–83; colonialist history of,
    99; drainage and development of, 2,
    15–17, 132–33, 135–37, 150; federal
    intervention in, 14–15; fire and, 56;
    human history of, 4, 26, 144; map of,
    vii, ix, 16, 97; mobility within, 76–
    79, 83, 86–88, 103; naming, 11, 25;
    nonhuman history of, 27; nostalgia
    for, 155; outlaw mythology of, 2;
    physical landscape of, 11–12, 25,
    46; predrainage, 11–12; restoration

of, 1, 4; as rhizome, 64; transformation of, 15–17; visions of, 1–2, 11–13, 34, 75; white settlement in, 10–11, 99. *See also* Comprehensive Everglades Restoration Plan; Everglades National Park; landscape

Everglades Agricultural Area, 17, 135–36

Everglades National Park, 15, 87, 95–97, 114, 154; establishment of, 135, 156

Everglades Wonder Gardens, 65

Fakahatchee Strand, 65

Farrel, Buster, 82–83

Fawcett, G. L., 109

Federal Writer's Project, 82, 133

fire, 2, 20, 32–33, 126, 142; hunting and, 55–59, 78; refrain of, 64, 153

Flagler, Henry, 13, 36, 38

Flamingo, village of, 82

flesh, 30, 32, 45, 59–65, 126. *See also* alligators; hide market

Florida Department of Game and Fresh Water Fish, 34–35, 174n17

Florida Game and Fresh Water Fish Commission (FGFC), 131–33, 137, 139, 140, 146–47, 174n17

Florida Wildlife, 139

Fontaneda, Hernando de Escalante, 5

game wardens, 57, 61, 87, 137–38, 140, 145

gator rods, 50–51, 53

Gifford, John C., 109

gladeland passageways, 88–89

Glades Culture, 5–6, 18

gladesmen, 2, 3, 28, 44; as criminals, 126; displacement of, 4–5, 17–18;

fire and, 56, 57–59; gendered language, 18–19; hunter's landscape of, 26–27, 138; hunting territories of, 32, 87–88; income activities of, 130; law and, 137, 138; mobility and, 32, 83–88; naming of, 18–20; in naturalist literature, 100, 101, 115–16, 119; nostalgia of, 25–26, 74; poaching and, 137, 138; resistance to the law, 139; rifles and, 52, 65; Royal Palm and, 113–14, 117; snakes and, 79; strategies of subversion, 35, 145–46; territories of, 142–44, 153. *See also* hunter's landscape; hunting

glades skiffs, 83–86

Gomez, John "Old Man Gomez," 81

Gramsci, Antonio, 145

Great Depression, 13

Griffin, Frank, 8

grunting, 59–60

Gumbo Limbo Trail, 97

hammocks, 12, 13, 96–97

Haraway, Donna, 28

Harney, William S., 8–9

Harper, Roland, 109

Hay, Douglas, 148

Heilner, Van Campen, 66

Hendrickson, Wilber, 154–55

Henshall, James, 81

Hermer, Joe, 119

hide market, 50, 59, 75, 132; impact of state regulation on, 126, 134–35, 138, 147–48; preparation for, 62–63, 127–28, 141–42; prices, 129–30, 133, 137, 146; Seminole participation in, 8, 10. *See also* alligator hunting

Hirsch, Eric, 27

Hogarth, Peter, 29
Hollander, Gail, 15
Hollander, Wolf, 81
Howell, Arthur, 109
Huffstodt, James T., 21, 137, 139
hunter's landscape, 26–27, 44, 83, 157;
commodification and, 125, 131; fire
and, 55–56; mobility and, 74, 79;
narrow escape and, 65–66; nonhuman effects on, 33; refrains
and, 47, 50, 64; rhizome and, 29,
32, 95; Royal Palm Hammock,
98; territorial practice and, 47, 59,
60, 66
hunting, 19–20, 114, 137; antihunting legislations, 137–38, 145;
market demand and, 44, 59; as
territorial practice, 31–32, 47,
59, 142–45

Indian Key massacre, 9–10

Jackson, Andrew, 8, 99
Jackson, Jack, 99
Jacoby, Karl, 117, 126
Joe River, 33, 155
Jonas, Susan, 80

Kadlec, David, 133
Kersey, Harry, 10
Kohler, Robert, 102, 110–13, 116–17
Kohn, Eduardo, 60

La Barre, Weston, 80
Lacey Act of 1900, 147, 150
Lake Okeechobee, 10, 11, 13, 21, 87
Lamb, John S., 18

landings, 87
landscape, 99, 153; discourse of, 83,
103; ecological significance of, 96;
of the Everglades, 1, 12–17, 88, 89,
95; indigenous people and, 101;
scholarly approaches to, 27–29,
74–76
"landscape ethnography," 28–29, 31
Latour, Bruno, 28, 33, 95, 101–3,
118–19
law, 131–35, 137. *See also* alligator
hunting; alligator protection laws
Le Billon, Philippe, 140–41
Lefebvre, Henri, 79
Leopold, Aldo, 96
Lévi-Strauss, Claude, 25
Little Laura and Big John (1973), 69,
70–71
Lodge, Thomas, 162n29
Low, Kid, 68
Loxahatchee National Wildlife
Refuge, 18
Lynn, Ray, 92, 121, 122

mangrove, 2, 12, 32, 95, 140, 143
masculinity, 19, 63
Mazzotti, F. J., 150
McCally, David, 12, 150
memory, 22, 26–28, 80, 83, 89–90,
143; nostalgia of glades hunters,
25–26, 74. *See also* hunter's
landscape
Miccosukees, 2–3
Middleton, Clarence, 68, 92, 121, 122
mimesis, 63–64
Mobley, Hanford, 69, 92, 121, 122, 154
Mobley, Wesley, 121, 155

mosquitoes, 85–86
Munroe, Kirk, 61, 107, 113
Musil, Robert, 73

Nabokov, Vladimir, 106
national park, 98, 99
naturalist literature, 119
nature, commodification of, 125–26
Neumann, Roderick, 99, 145
Nissenson, Marilyn, 80

Okeechobee Fruit Lands Company,
  12–13
Old Ingraham Highway, 117
Orlove, Ben, 18
outlaw mythology, 2
Overstreet, LeRoy, 52

Padgett, Norman, 21
Padgett, Oren B. "O. B.," 39–40, 91,
  120, 121
Panther Key, 81, 82
Perrine, Henry, 9–10
Pickering, Andrew, 34
Piper brothers, 65
poaching, 139, 144, 145–46, 148, 156
politics of naturalization, 95–96
"politics of nature," 3, 32–33, 95
Powers, Lige, 85, 88
Proveti, John, 33, 45
Pyne, Stephen J., 55

"Queen of the Everglades." See
  Upthegrove, Laura

Ralston, Walter, 81
"reclamation," 1, 12

red mangrove, 29–30, 89–90
Reese, Albert, 129, 149
refrain, 45–46, 59, 64. See also earth;
  fire; flesh
reterritorialization, 47
rhizome, 35, 45, 64, 88, 90, 153;
  definition of, 29–31
Riblett, Robert, 154, 155
Robbins, Paul, 28
Roberts, Steve, 82
Roberts Lake, 147
Robertson, William B., 56
Rodgers, Edmond, 38, 40
Rolfs, Peter Henry, 109
Royal Palm Hammock, 95–96, 97, 106,
  119; discovery of, 103–6; field history of, 107–8, 110, 117; gladesmen
  and, 115–16, 117–18; human history
  of, 98–99, 100, 102; as a landscape of
  ecological significance, 98, 99–100,
  101–2, 108–10, 117; naming of, 118;
  natural history of, 100; residential
  knowledge and, 113–14; scientific
  knowledge of, 113–14, 117; Seminole inhabitation of, 99, 113, 115,
  117–18; social history of, 114–15;
  survey of, 101. See also tropics
Royal Palm State Park, 108, 118

Safford, W. E., 101, 109, 110
Schama, Simon, 27–28, 88
science, 95, 98, 100
Scott, James, 145
Seminoles, 2–3, 5, 61, 96, 104, 161n;
  Bill Ashley and, 155; canoes of,
  83–84; naturalists' inclusion of,
  115, 119; Royal Palm and, 106–7.

Whidden, H. Pete, 19, 65, 143; alligator hunting and, 48–49, 52–53,
55, 63, 78
Whiskey Creek, 87, 88
white settlement, 5
wilderness, 17, 71, 99, 101, 110;
conservation and, 2, 4, 126
wildlife management, 132, 133, 137

Williams, Ada Coats, 68, 155,
163n
Williams, Archie, 11, 81
Willoughby, Hugh deLaussett, 77,
82, 85, 98, 102; surveying efforts
of, 103–6, 115, 118
Wilson, E. O., 80
women, 19–20

Laura A. Ogden is associate professor of anthropology at Florida International University. She has conducted fieldwork in the Florida Everglades for the past decade and is coauthor (with Glen Simmons) of *Gladesmen: Gator Hunters, Moonshiners, and Skiffers.*